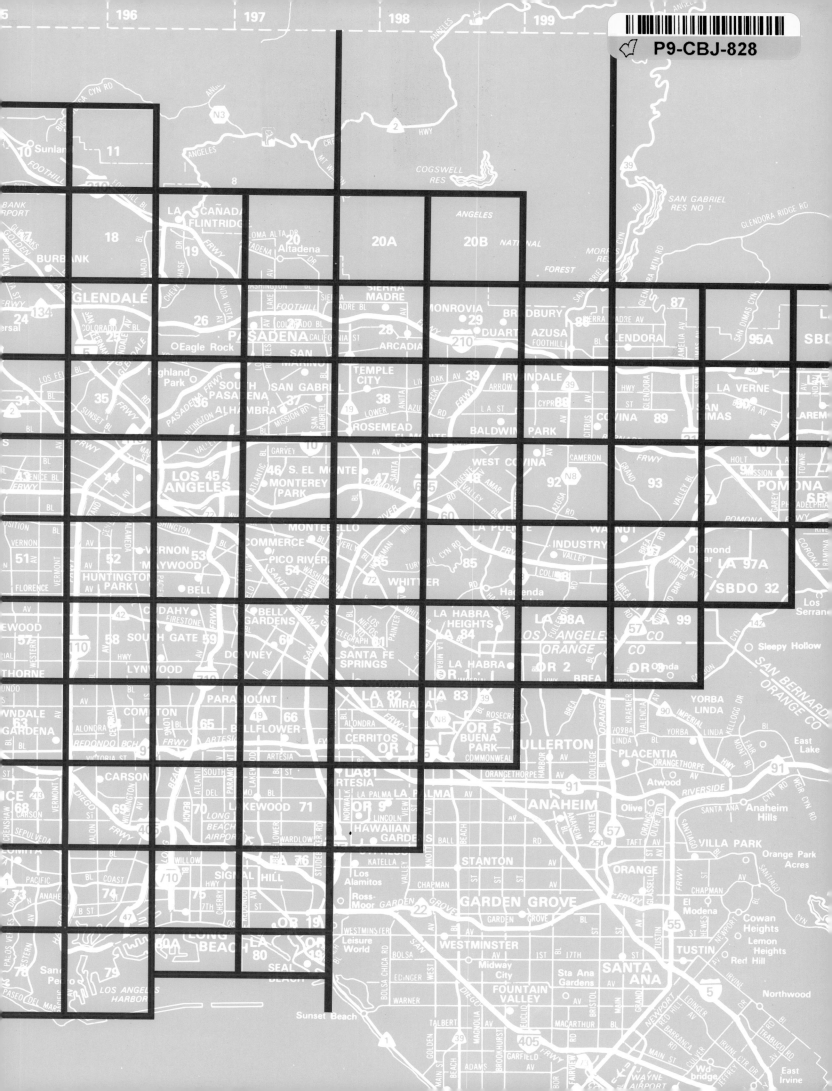

GRAPHIC DESIGN

Los Angeles

Designed and edited by
Gerry Rosentswieg

Written by
Julie Prendiville

Introduction by
Saul Bass

Published by
Madison Square Press

ISBN 0-8230-4891-8
Library of Congress Catalog Card Number   88-61410

Distributors to the trade in the United States and Canada:
Watson-Guptill Publications 1515 Broadway, New York, N.Y. 10036

Distributed throughout the rest of the world:
Hearst Books International 105 Madison Avenue, New York, N.Y. 10016

Publisher:
Madison Square Press
10 East 23rd Street, New York, N.Y. 10010

Designer/Editor: Gerry Rosentswieg

Printed in Japan

CONTENTS

photo: John Livzey

It is an opportunity to see, compare and evaluate the graphic design in Los Angeles—the large studios and the small, the well-established studios headed by designers who have shaped the industry and the new ones who are changing that shape.

Actually, there is no "L.A. style." Los Angeles graphic design studios are diverse, ranging from very corporate to very playful, from a fine art orientation to machine-created images. Sometimes all in the same piece. Each studio represented here has its own design bias. They are all different. They are all good.

Los Angeles is a huge city—as large as some countries—with a sprawling network of inadequate freeways that make it difficult to get to work and almost impossible to service clients. An hour drive home after work is not unusual.

In contrast, Los Angeles is situated on a picturesque bend of the Pacific coast. It is sunny, warm and full of light. Swimming in the ocean in December and skiing nearby until early summer are very real possibilities. Los Angeles is a city full of art, entertainment and distraction, where free time is easy to fill.

For all these reasons, Los Angeles does not foster a system of professional networking. In fact, it promotes a professional isolation. This isolation allows design studios to develop personal attitudes and style. It is this personal style that characterizes the graphic design of Los Angeles.

In the months preceding the 1984 Olympic games, with time running out, the Los Angeles Olympic Organizing Committee decided to use a group of design studios to accomplish the many print and environmental projects required. Many of the studios in this book were a part of that team. During that period, there was an unprecedented interchange in the Los Angeles design offices. That interchange created a sense of community. That sense of community prompted this book.

Gerry Rosentswieg
4-25-88

Someone once said that if you lifted up the United States on the East Coast, everything that wasn't nailed down would slide into California. And has.

Of course California's greatest period of explosive growth occurred during the years just after World War II. The troops who passed through Southern California on the way to and from the Far East decided that if they had one life to live, it was better to live it here than in Cleveland. And it was one wave of refugees after another, from the East Coast, mid-West, Latin and Central America, and Asia.

I have a personal theory about the post-war colonization of Southern California. Every year on January 1st, millions of Americans are hung over. Outside the snow is higher than an elephant's privates. It's 18 degrees out and overcast. Then they turn on the television and see thousands of people sitting in bright Pasadena sunlight wearing short-sleeved shirts. And terrific looking Pac Ten cheerleaders doing back flips in skimpy outfits.

I believe the Rose Bowl has brought more people to Los Angeles than Greyhound.

New York, Chicago, Boston, even Cleveland were mature markets. Businesses there were mature businesses fed by old-world cultural traditions. More often than not, the people running things were professional managers.

In Los Angeles, on the other hand, there were a whole pot full of businesses that were founded by people who came here after the war. These people weren't professional managers. They were entrepreneurial, innovative, risk-takers. People who were personally involved with their products. Wine, toys, foods, cosmetics, airplanes, computers.

You know, working with people who start things, who create things is very different than working with people who manage things. In good ways and bad. Entrepreneurial clients are

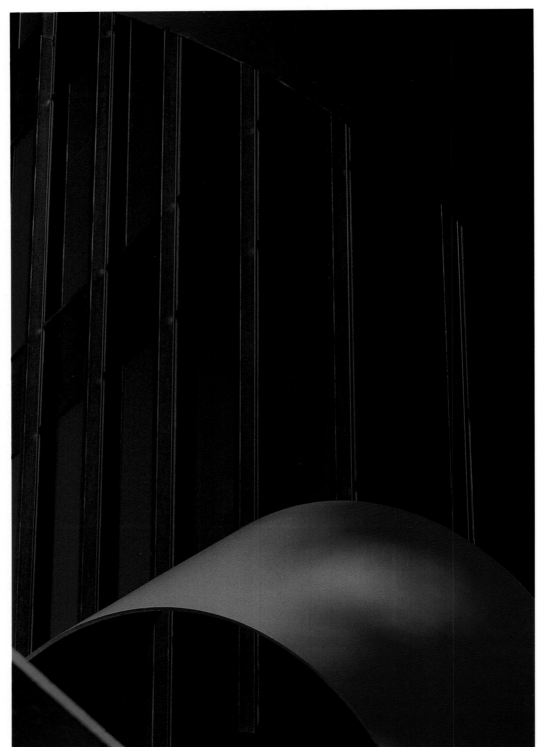

usually more emotional, arbitrary, risk-oriented, instinctive. Professional managers are more objective, rational, and have better manners and nicer clothes.

The design market in Los Angeles has historically been a very tough one and it continues to get tougher. Designers like living here. I don't blame them, so do I. Some designers believe that it's easier to sell great work here than in New York. I'm not sure I agree. To do great work, great clients are essential and they seem to pop up in the most unlikely places, even, on occasions, New York.

What I value most out here is the quality and quantity of the light. As much as I love New York, if I spend too much time there when the weather is crumby, I get depressed.

The fact that so many of the large design firms have opened or are planning to open offices in Los Angeles is only partially in response to the fact that Los Angeles is now the second largest market in the country. Equally as important is that things are happening here. Exciting things. We have been a style center, for example, movies, television, fashion, music, food, for a long time.
I have another personal theory. We'll probably never know if I'm right, but I believe the real reason so many of our colleagues are opening offices out here is that it gives them a tax deductible reason to get away from East Coast winters.

Saul Bass
4-25-88

…gias Joseph

1250 Sixth Street
Suite 201

Santa Monica
California

90401

213 458 1899

BesserJosephPartners

Graphic Design

Cross Associates

Designers

James A. Cross
President

10513 W. Pico Boulevard
Los Angeles, CA 90064
Te…
1484

Dave Williamson & Associates

8800 Venice Boulevard
Los Angeles,
California 90034
Phone 213/836-0143

Dave Williamson

Gerry Rosentswieg/The Graphics Studio

Corporate and
Institutional
Communications

811 North Highland Avenue
Los Angeles, California 90038
Telephone 213.466.2666

Tracey Shiffman   Roland Young

Design Group

7421 Beverly Boulevard
Suites 4 & 5
Los Angeles, CA 90036

Telephones:
213 930-1816
213 930-1873

793-7847

Wayne
Hunt
Graphic
Design

87 N. Raymond Ave
#215
Pasadena
3

The Bradbury Building, Suite 438
304 South Broadway,
Los Angeles, California 90013
687-7422

GEM/F&C

Grey Entertainment & Media
1119 Colorado Avenue
Suite 104
Santa Monica, CA 90401
…3 458-9499

BUTLER
KOSH
BROOKS

9 4 0 N O R T H
H I G H L A N D
S U I T E C
L O S A N G E L E S
C A 9 0 0 3 8
2 1 3 4 6 9 8 1 2 8

Rod Dyer
Group, Inc.
Design &
Advertising

8360 Melrose Ave.
3rd Floor
Los Angeles
CA 90069
213 655-1800
FAX 213 655-9159

…yama Production Manager

Since its beginning, forty-one years ago, Advertising Designers, Inc. has had a goal: to retain design control by not getting too big. "When a design firm grows too large," contends president Tom Ohmer, "it can lose its creative spark."

So even though AD has captured many times the amount of business they had ten years ago, the staff remains less than ten people.

"We must be working smarter, because we still play on the weekends," smiles Ohmer.

Projects vary widely at this design office. Pinned to the wall of the conference room, one may see roughs for an annual report concept, a corporate identity program, package design, or an ad campaign at any given time. AD designs for large, international corporations and small, fledgling companies. "We have a good mix of clients in many areas, and that keeps it intriguing," says Ohmer.

1

2

1. Bruce Dobson and Tom Ohmer.
2. Self-promotion kit. "How we can help you...toot your own horn."
3. Annual report for City National Corporation.
4. Capabilities brochure for Tower Metallurgical Group.

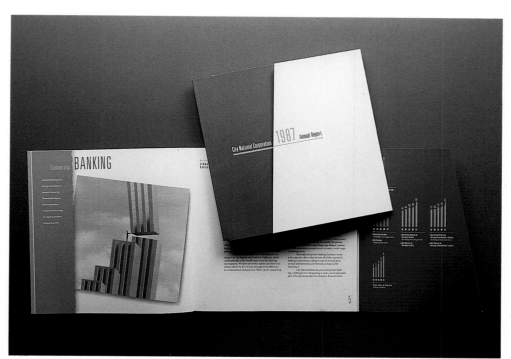

3

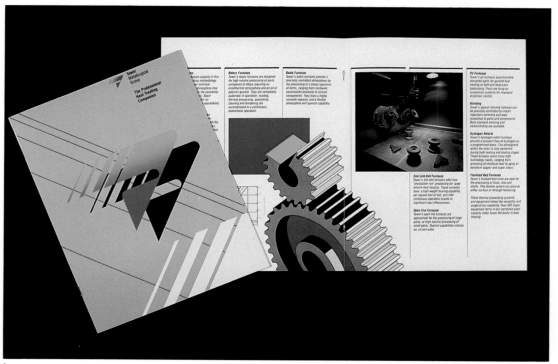

4

1. + 8. Symbol for Great American
Bank.
2. Symbol for Foodcraft.
3. Symbol for Tower Industries, Inc.,
Metal Fabricators.
4. Symbol for House of Fabrics, Inc.
5. Symbol for Commercial Interior
Services, Inc.
6. Symbol for Fred Sands Realtors.
7. Symbol for First Regional Bank.
9. Symbol for City National Bank.
10. Brochure for ANCO, an engineering
firm.
11. Forecast brochure for First
Interstate Bank of California.
12. Brochure for CalComp System 25.
13. Annual report for Stars to Go,
merchandisers of video rentals.
14. Annual report for Pauley
Petroleum.

2

3

4

5

6

7

8

9

1

10

11

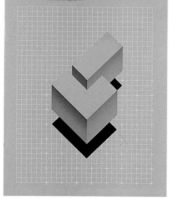

12

13

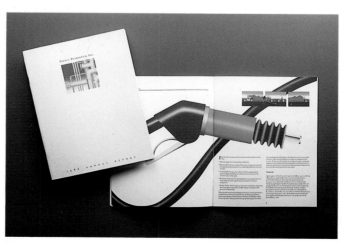

14

1

1. Real estate brochure for Mission Grove.
2. Call-for-entries poster for computer art competition.
3. Institutional package for Foodcraft coffee.
4. Product brochure for CalComp.
5. Packaging for Graphic Solutions, a series of manuals.
6. Advertisement and check design for Bankprint.

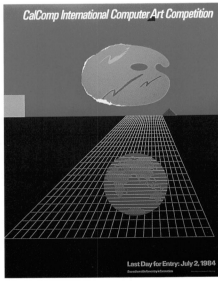

2

3

4

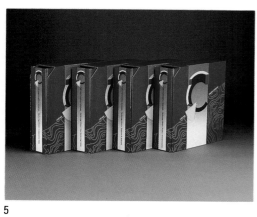

5

6

1

1. Annual report for Pauley Petroleum.
2. Annual report for Kerr-McGee Corporation.
3. Packaging and product design for Calorie Glass.

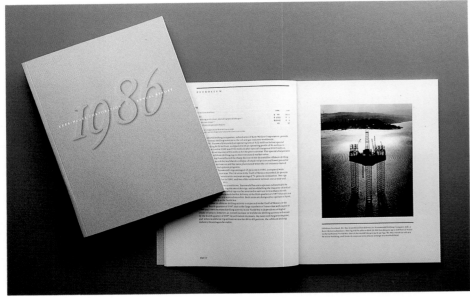

2

3

Young in years, innovative in attitude and approach, Antista Design is always looking for new ways to create. "We don't use preconceived formulae for design or running a design business," says founder Tom Antista.

In packaging, posters, collateral materials, identity programs and special projects, this fast-growing firm is always striving for solutions that represent, above all, design excellence. For their diverse client base the result is original and effective communication materials.

"It's important for our studio to have a style, a look," explains Antista. "How it evolves during the design process becomes very exciting for us and for our clients. That enthusiasm is always apparent in the end result."

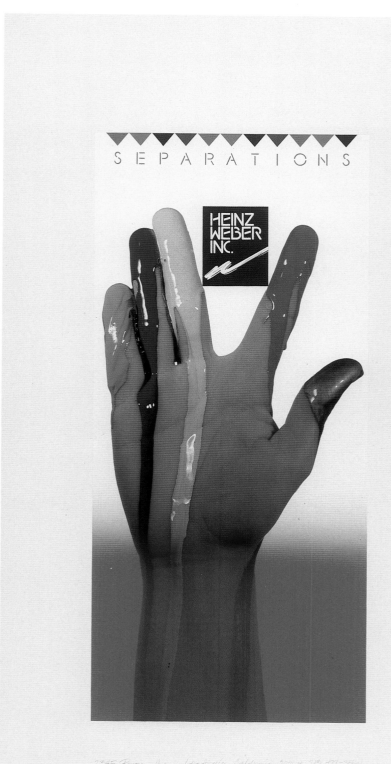

1. Design staff: (l. to r.) Lee Fukui, Thomas Fairclough, Eric Nakamura, Petrula Vrontikis, Tom Antista, not pictured Paula Cruz and Robert Garcia.
2. Self-portrait by Tom Antista.
3. Promotional poster for a color separation house.

1

1. Poster for a silkscreen printing
competition.
2. + 3. Real estate leasing brochure for
Colorado Place.
4. Brochure for Southern California
Gas Co. "The Elements of Enhanced
Energy Efficiency."

2

COLORADO PLACE PHASE I

If another measure of concrete or steel had never been added to the original Colorado Place, it would stand as a superlative achievement as a superior Santa Monica business center.

Its trio of three-story buildings is architecturally noteworthy. Its 500,000 square feet of office and retail space have received enthusiastic tenant acceptance.

Its terraces, atriums, multi-level landscaped parking, and park-like setting are a refreshing contrast to mid-city towers.

Its success has been marked by a high degree of both recognition and visability.

COLORADO PLACE PHASE II

In the step-by-step evolution of its unfolding master plan, Colorado Place has expanded into a new second phase: Colorado Place North.

Colorado Place North, under construction, will add to the total Colorado Place concept three mid-rise office buildings providing a total of approximately 541,000 additional square feet of office space; one six-story of 166,000 square feet and a five-story of 145,000 square feet. The third building also will be five-stories of approximately 230,000 square feet. It will be graced by a more than three-acre recreational park, picturesque terraces, a luxury subterranean first-run cinema complex and ample parking.

THE TOTAL COLORADO PLACE CONCEPT

Taken individually, Colorado Place and Colorado Place North each would stand high on the roster of most desirable business addresses. Architecturally congruent, together they combine to be an unsurpassed business center choice.

Because the whole is greater than the sum of its parts, the original Colorado Place, now joined by Colorado Place North, achieves true greatness. Through this process of synergism, all those who share the Colorado Place address will enjoy the advantages of this positive incremental growth.

3

4

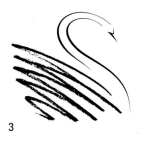

1

2

3

4

5

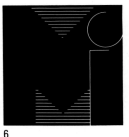

6

LAZERTONE

7

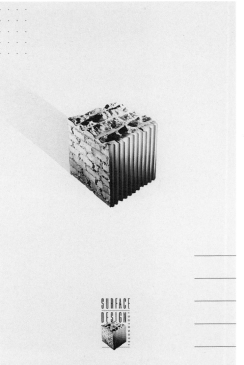

8

1. Symbol for You-Nique, importers of Italian shoes.
2. Logotype for Voyou, fashion importers.
3. Symbol for a Bullock's Department Store grand opening promotion.
4. Symbol for Heritage Museum, Utah.
5. Symbol for copywriter Aileen Farnan Antonier.
6. Symbol for Max Imports, Jewelry.
7. Logotype for Lazertone, a graphics production house.
8.+12. Product brochure for Surface Design Technology.
9. Product catalog for Surface Design Technology.
10.+11. Exhibit design and detail for R.D. Olson, Construction.

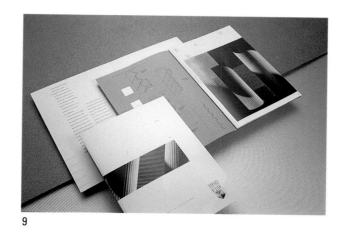

9

10

11

12

to using surfaces... for unique environmental illusions

A new dimension in realism That will change your approach.

Surface Design Technology manufactures unique surface materials used in the creation of environmental illusions. Using expanded technology and expertise once the exclusive domain of major movie studios, Surface Design offers cost-effective and time-efficient methods for creating distinctive film and theatrical scenery, retail displays, trade show environments, and countless other applications.

Surface Design materials can transform large flat or curved surfaces into durable, dimensional settings of brick, stone,

Surface Design Technology's experience as a supplier for the entertainment industry has enabled us to structure our quality-craft to the challenges and rapid pace of commercial advertising, film, and theatre. Efficient, versatile, and inventive solutions to developing our products and satisfying a very demanding clientele are the result.

rock, and various other textures with a series of simple steps. The care and attention that go into these designs and the hand-crafted manufacture process of the surfaces assure a high quality product with incomparable realism.

Surface Design products are hybrid polyester resin cast sheets of flexible fiberglass-reinforced plastic. This unique material is able to be cut and applied with ordinary wood fabricating tools. The material also gives the surfaces durability and an inherent shatter-resistance, making them excellent for most

Cast resin appliques, such as rivets and bolt heads add interesting, effective detail to any surface.

uses on walls and floors. The surfaces have interlocking register patterns to avoid the straight-line seams of conventional wall panelling. The sheets are delivered ready for immediate application and painting.

Surface Design Technology's manufacturing facility in Southern California has a large inventory and a wide distribution network for your convenience. A product catalogue is available for more information on the scope of our product line, technical data, and instructions for use.

This popular attraction was constructed with the use of Surface Design materials. Photo: Lexington Scenery & Props

Surface Design Technology generated molds and produced custom designed wall surfaces for the San Francisco Opera's new production of "Fidelio". Photo: Ron Scherl

Along with surface material sheet goods and cast resin appliques, our product line includes architectural details, flexible molding, and special industrial elements.

· ·

1427 Santa Monica Mall, Suite 206   Santa Monica, CA 90401   213/393-1352 FAX: 213/395-9437

1

2

1. Package design for Wolfgang
Puck Food Co., frozen foods.
2. Package design program for
You-Nique.

BASS/YAGER & ASSOCIATES

Saul Bass, graphic designer and film-maker, Oscar award nominee and winner, has had monumental impact on the field of graphic design. Work he has done has changed the field.

His firm, Bass/Yager & Associates, creates corporate identity programs, packaging and environmental design for domestic and international companies and corporations.

Herb Yager remembers a question he asked Saul some years back. He asked his partner, "If you had a lot of money and could do whatever you wanted, what would it be?"

"I have a lot of money," replied Saul. "And I'm doing it."

1

2

1. Poster for "The Man With the Golden Arm."
2. Saul Bass.
3. Poster for AT&T.
4. Symbol for AT&T.
5. Symbol for Celanese.
6. Environmental sculpture of Celanese symbol.
7. Poster introducing new symbol for Girl Scouts of America.

3

4

CELANESE

5

The new face of Girl Scouting

GIRL SCOUTS

7

6

1

2

1. Aircraft marking and symbol
for United Airlines.
2. Aircraft marking and symbol
for Continental Airlines.
3. Modular design for new and
remodeled stations for Exxon.
4. Station design for Gulf
branded stations.
5.+6. Symbol and application
for Rockwell International.

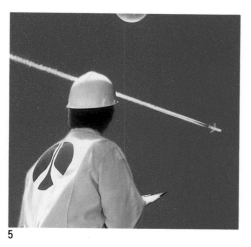

5

3

Rockwell International

6

4

1

2

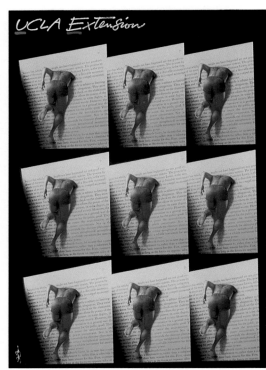

3

1. Packaging for AT&T.
2. Poster for the Los Angeles Music Center.
3. Poster promoting U.C.L.A. Extension courses.
4. Packaging and symbol for Lawry's Foods.
5. Symbol for United Way.

4

5

7039 W. Sunset Blvd.   Los Angeles, CA 90028   213/466-9701 FAX: 213/466-9700

2

3

4

1. Poster for Bass' film "Why Man Creates."
2.-4. Scenes from "Quest," a film directed by Saul and Elaine Bass.
5. Poster for the Los Angeles International Film Exposition (Filmex).

1

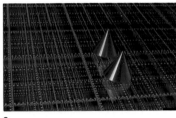

5

BESSER JOSEPH PARTNERS

From small, private companies to large public corporations, Besser Joseph Partners enjoys a diverse clientele in fields including high technology, financial services, entertainment, real estate development, health services, consumer products and education. For these clients the firm designs print, packaging, identity and environmental communications.

Rik Besser and Doug Joseph are graduates of the Art Center College of Design where they met over ten years ago. Both are members of the Art Center faculty and teach annual report design. They see an exciting future for graphic designers.

"In five years, Los Angeles is going to be a whole different design community," says Rik. "I think it's great for companies like ours."

1

2

3

4

1. Rik Besser, Doug Joseph
2.-4. Annual report for Dep
Corporation, manufacturers of
personal care products.

1

4

2

5

3

6

1.-3. Annual report for Avery, specialty adhesive manufacturer.
4.-6. Annual report for National Semiconductor Corporation.
7. Package design for Vuarnet eyewear treatment product.
8. Package design for Nissan Vacuum bottle.
9. Point-of-purchase display for Vuarnet sunglasses.
10. Package design for Vuarnet sunglasses.

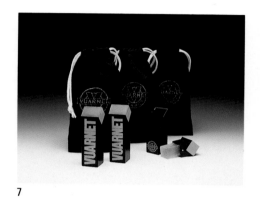

7

8

9

10

1

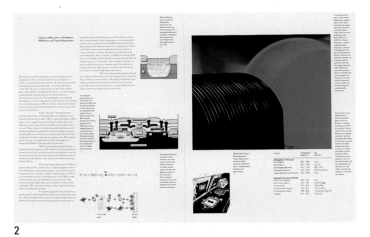

2

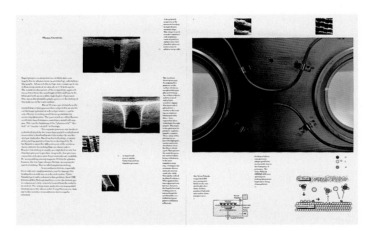

6

1.-3. Annual report for Tylan
Corporation, a semi-conductor
equipment manufacturer.
4.-6. Corporate databook for National
Semiconductor Corporation.
7. Internal poster for National
Semiconductor Corporation.
8. Internal poster for Lockheed.
9.-11. Annual report for Avery.

9

10

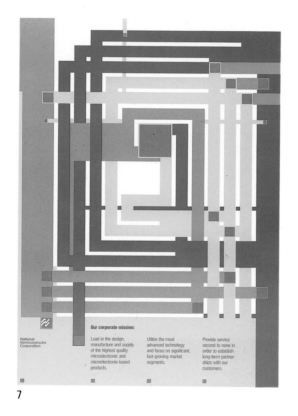

7

11

8

BESSER JOSEPH PARTNERS

···

1250 Sixth Street, Suite 201   Santa Monica, CA 90401   213/458-1899 FAX: 213/394-1789

1

1.-3. Annual report for Lincoln Bancorp.

2

3

44

"For a look into the future of corporate identity and symbol design, open your wallet, look at a credit card, and examine the colored hologram," says Doug Boyd. "These holograms reflect new and exciting technologies emerging which will help designers develop totally new images for their clients."

And Douglas Boyd Design and Marketing wants to be there. Whether the project calls for a single brochure or a full identity program, this firm believes it's imperative to keep pace with marketing and design innovations.

Founded in 1970, the firm is located on Melrose Avenue near the Pacific Design Center. "It's a dynamic street," Doug says. "It's full of design, innovation, color and excitement."

1

2

3

4

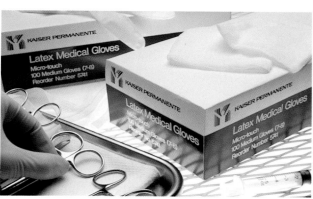

5

6

1. Doug Boyd at Aesthedes computer.
2. Exhibit poster for N.Y. Art Directors Club Show which Boyd sponsored in Los Angeles.
3.-7. Corporate identity program for Kaiser Permanente, a health maintenance organization.

7

1

1.+2. Retail environment design for FINA.
3. Poster for ARCO Solar.
4. Sales support material for Arco Solar.
5.+6. Package design for Apple Computer.
7. Packaging system for Revell.
8.+9. Logotype and packaging for Toys International.

2

3

4

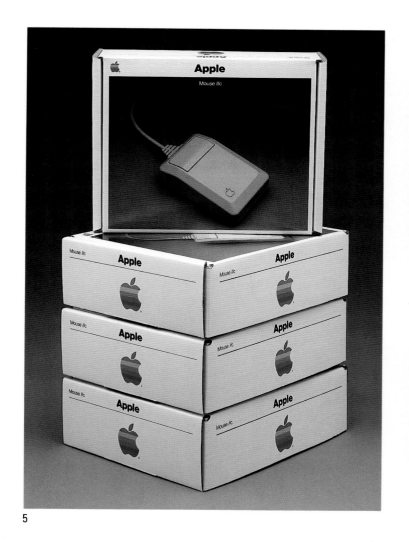

5

7

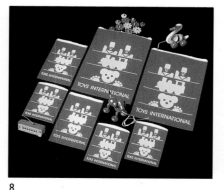

8

9

6

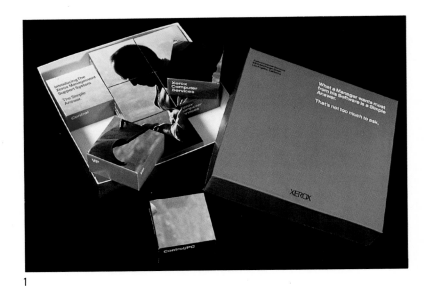

1

2

3

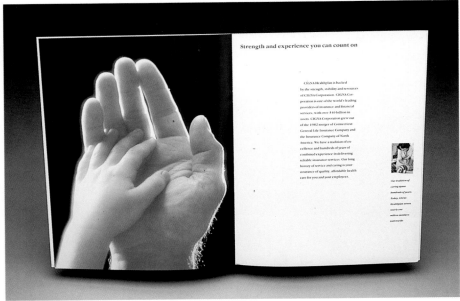

4

5

1. Promotional package for Xerox Corporation.
2. Sales brochure for Xerox Corporation.
3. + 4. Brochure system for CIGNA, Healthplan.
5. Packaging program for a bakery.
6.-8. Signage for Fox Plaza, Los Angeles.
9. + 10. Signage for the City of Brea, California.

6

7

8

9

10

6624 Melrose Avenue   Los Angeles, CA 90038   213/655-9642 FAX: 213/655-9649

1

2

3

4

1.-4. Logotype and packaging system for Revell.
5. + 6. Promotional package and sculpture for DesignWeave.

5

6

52

"Design is largely a problem-solving process of bringing order to chaos," says Keith Bright.

Since 1977, Bright & Associates has brought order to clients involved in the business of banking to tourism to computers to beer, in the form of corporate identity, packaging, collateral materials and environmental design.

The Los Angeles Olympics of 1984 was a great moment for Bright & Associates. The firm was tagged for some of the major design projects for the games; two programs, in particular, were the pictograms and the gargantuan official report; two large volumes which weighed in at a hefty 38 lbs. With clients in Japan and New Zealand, Bright's work in corporate communications is recognized all over the world.

Looking ahead, Bright & Associates sees the need for better mass market packaging and is eagerly looking for opportunities. With over 45 staff members, Keith has managed to develop a well-organized design and marketing firm that will continue to make its mark far into the future.

1

3

2

55

4

5

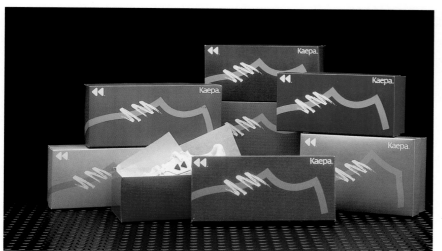

6

7

8

1. A collection of models and prototypes from the studio.
2. Bright & Associates staff.
3. Keith Bright.
4. Package design for yogurt.
5. Pictograms designed for the 1984 Summer Olympics in Los Angeles.
6.-7. Packaging program and symbol for athletic shoes.
8. Package design for frozen food.

1

1. Press kit and stationery system for Sail America's bid for The America's Cup '88 competition.
2. Symbol for Sail America.
3. Package design for Ashton-Tate software.
4.+9. Symbol and application for Coast Savings.
5.+ 7. Symbol and application for National Car Rental.
6.+8. Symbol and application for Host International.
10. Symbol for Ashton-Tate software.

2

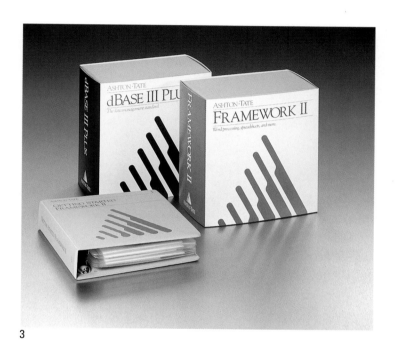

3

7

8

9

10

4

5

6

57

1

1. Packaging system for a candy company.
2. Packaging for Olympia Brewery.
3. Sales materials for eyewear.
4. Application of symbol for Andresen Typographics.
5. Logotype for Citrus, a Los Angeles restaurant.
6. Symbol for New Zealand Steel.
7. Symbol for Fox Broadcasting.
8. Symbol for Burlington Air Express.
9. Symbol for "The Californias" campaign promoting tourism.

2

3

4

5

6

7

8

9

1. Identity program for Holland
America Cruise Line.
2. Self-promotional gift package.

There's a current of high-charged energy running through the design firm of Butler, Kosh, Brooks, fueled mostly by its three founders.

Craig Butler, Kosh and Larry Brooks are designers who are infectiously enthusiastic about what they do. "We're trying to do something better than anybody else," says Butler. All three are directly involved in the firm's projects, each bringing a different area of expertise to the job.

Involved in the entertainment, automotive and consumer products industries, the firm designs corporate identity programs, collateral pieces, advertising and packaging programs, along with movie posters.

Of their design philosophy, Kosh says, "We encourage the client to take the next step, to push the barriers. What is sensational today is boring next week."

1

2

1. Art Deco building which houses the firm.
2. Interior of studio.
3. Paper company promotion for Champion paper featuring portraits by photographer, Tom Zimberoff.
4. Poster introducing a new car model for Isuzu.

3

4

1

2

3

4

5

6

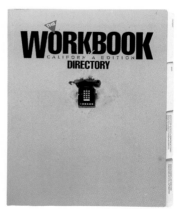

7

8

9

10

11

12

13

1.-10. Covers for The Workbook, a compendium designed for The Graphic Arts Industry.
10.-13. Boxed package for the 10th Volume of The Workbook and the individual covers for the component parts.
14. Promotional logotype for Butler, Kosh & Brooks.

14

1

2

3

4

5

6

1. Symbol for Walt Disney Home Video.
2. Symbol for Warren Z, women's clothing manufacturing company.
3. Symbol for Catchit, a surfwear manufacturing company.
4. Logotype for a television series.
5. Logotype and billboard application for a radio station.
6. Symbol for the LA Workbook.
7. Identity program for A & I, a photographic color lab.
8. Advertisement for eyewear.
9. Advertisement for sunglasses.
10. Promotional logotype for Butler, Kosh & Brooks.

7

8

MIRA

Mira the sunwear that combines space-age technology with a great fashion look, 100% UV and IR protection, anti-reflection coating on both front and back, protection from short wavelength blue light, scratch resistant, over 20 micro thin coatings that reflect harmful rays without giving up true color.

9

10

1

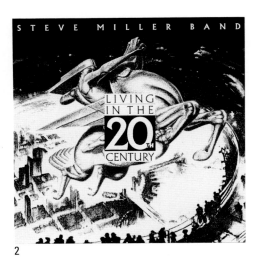

2

1. Promotional logotype for Butler, Kosh & Brooks.
2. Album cover for Capitol Records.
3. Album design for Electra Asylum.
4. Album cover for Warner Communications Inc.

3

4

JOHN CLEVELAND, INC.

John Cleveland believes good communication is just as important as good design. "There's a lot of design out there that's beautiful, but grossly irresponsible. As pretty as it is, it just does not communicate."

Since 1969, it has been John Cleveland's wish to get the message across. His vehicle is mainly the annual report, although the firm also handles visual identity programs and other projects.

Whether an assignment is for a product or a service, the purpose is the same. As John says, "We're not satisfied until and unless we contribute to the success of our clients."

1

2

3

4

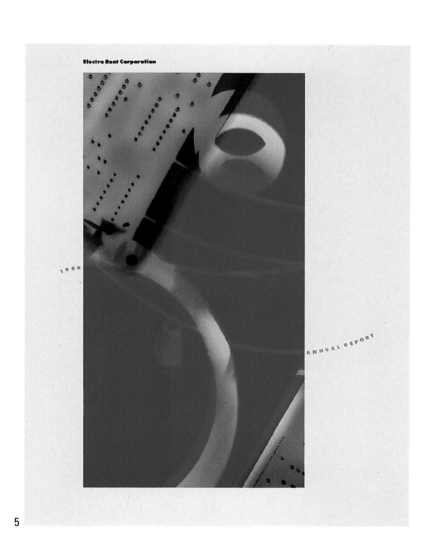

5

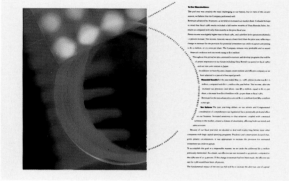

6

7

8

1.-4. Brochure documenting new ideas
in annual reports for S.D. Warren Co.
5.-8. Annual report for Electro Rent
Corporation.

1.-3. Annual report for The W.M. Keck Foundation.
4.-7. Annual report for Amgen, Inc., a biochemical pharmaceutical company.

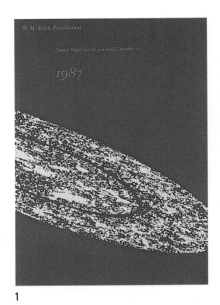

1

2

3

4

5

6

7

Southern
California
Graphics

8432
Steller
Drive

Culver City
California
90230

Telephone
213
559-3600

1

2

3

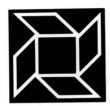

4

5

6

7

8

9

10

1. Logotype for a printer.
2. Symbol for Allied Corrugated Box Company.
3. Symbol for AstroData, manufacturers of circuit boards.
4. Symbol for American Telecommunications Corporation.
5. Symbol for Institute of Trichology, manufacturers of hair care products.
6. Symbol for Creative Capital Corporation.
7. Symbol for International Golf Travel.
8. Symbol for Power Products Inc.
9. Symbol for Edward Ellis Co., developers.
10.-12. Annual report for Tandon Corporation, manufacturers of miniaturized hardware for computers (with diagrams illustrating the product in use).

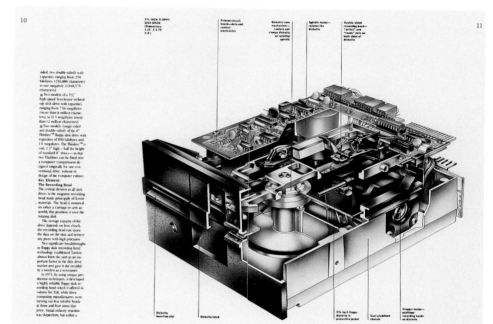

11

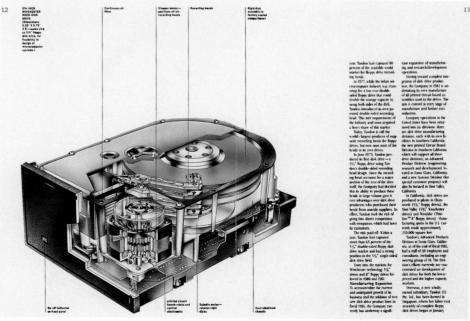

12

JOHN CLEVELAND, INC.

11611 San Vicente Blvd.   Los Angeles, CA 90049   213/826-0948 FAX: 213/826-5260

1.-5. Brochure, "Annual Report Trends" for S.D. Warren Co.

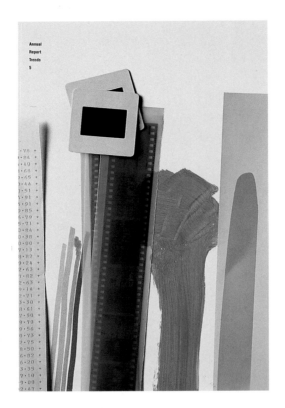

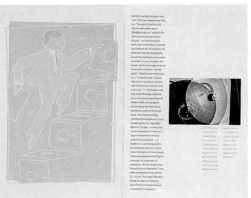

2

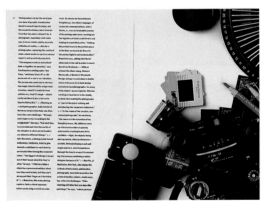

3

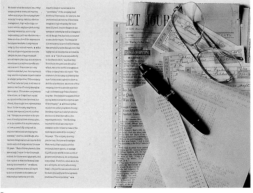

4

5

CORPORATE COMMUNICATIONS GROUP

Don Kano and Bruce Russell have built more than just a graphic design studio— CCG is a full-service, fully-staffed corporate communications group. From incisive annual reports to cogent corporate profiles to dynamic marketing communications.

"Our designers speak the language of Wall Street. Our writers speak the language of graphic design. Our group bridges the two, creating themes that unify and give meaning—and value—to our communications," explains Don Kano.

Their clients span the country and reach into Canada, Europe and Japan—all seeking integrated and powerful visual and verbal solutions. At CCG, communication succeeds—by design.

1

1. The Corporate Communications Group.
2.-4. Annual report for Farmers Group, Inc.

2

3

4

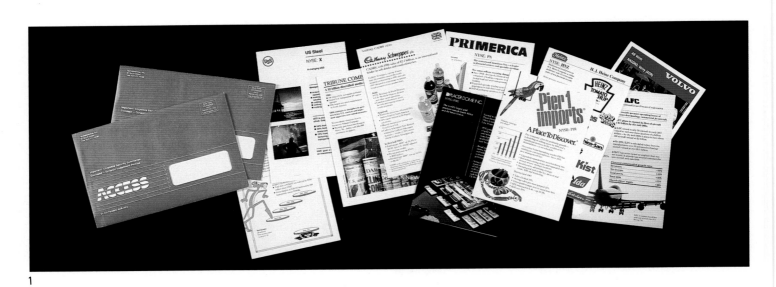

1

2

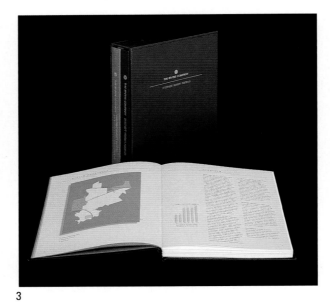

3

4

5

6

8

1. Direct mail financial profiles for publicly owned corporations.
2. Brochure for Westridge School.
3. Book for The Irvine Company.
4. Symbol for Personal Care Corporation.
5. Monogram for Universal Health Services.
6. Catalog for a furniture manufacturer.
7.-9. Brochure for Technimetrics.
10. Symbol for Hutton Associates, a commercial land development company.
11. Symbol for the Senate of Priests, Archdiocese of Los Angeles.

10

11

9

1

2

3

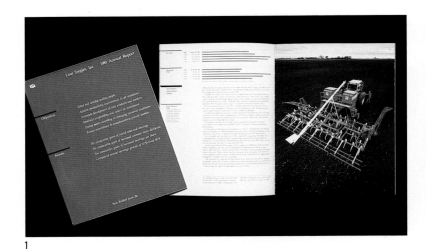

4

5

6

7

1. Annual report for Lear Siegler, Inc.
2. Annual report for International
Lease Finance Corporation.
3. + 4. Annual report for Phone Mate,
Inc.
5. + 6. Annual report for Hal Roach
Studios, Inc.
7. + 8. Annual report for Maxicare
.Health Plan, Inc.
9. Annual report for Caesar's Palace.

8

9

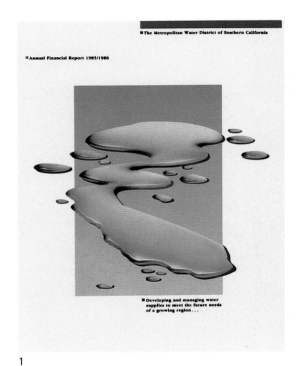

1

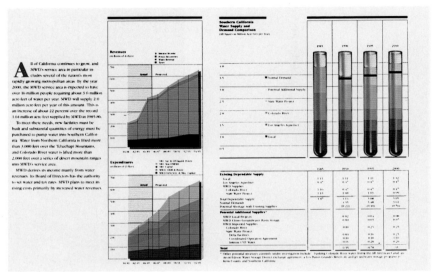

2

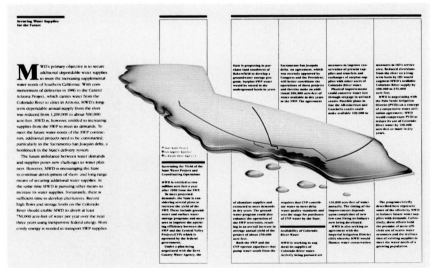

3

1.-3. Annual report for The Metropolitan
Water District of Southern California.

COY, LOS ANGELES

Coy is a fifteen-person studio principaled by John Coy, creative director, and Margaret Coy, executive director. At first you might not recognize a COY design. Chameleon-like, they seek to tailor each job to match its environment, calling attention to the key function of a piece more than promoting a particular style.

Style, however, is important at COY, as is wit and charm. They are fond of serving up playful with intelligent, formal with organic, thought-provoking with humorous …with a love for the classical and a penchant for the avant garde.

The COY client list ranges from fine art museums, educational institutions, interior design and furnishing manufacturers to paper companies, real estate developers and high-tech fundraisers. "Our clients are all artists of one sort or another," Coy says, "We want to reveal that artful nature in their graphics."

COY

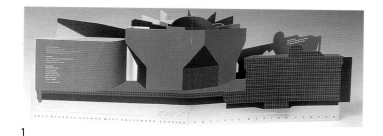

1

1. Leasing brochure in the shape of the
space for rent. Pacific Design Center,
Los Angeles.
2. Identity package for San Diego
Design Center.
3. Packaging design for Quady Winery.

2

3

1. Self-promotion poster for a lithographer.
2. Symbol for South Coast Metro, a business and cultural community.
3. Logotype for a hospital.
4. Symbol celebrating 25 years of programs.
5. + 7. Logotype for The Los Angeles Music Center Opera.
6. Logotype for B. Aubergine, limited edition wearables.

SOUTH COAST METRO

2

ChildrensHospitalLosAngeles

3

TWENTY FIVE YEARS OF THE ARTS
UCLA COLLEGE OF FINE ARTS

4

5

6

7

1

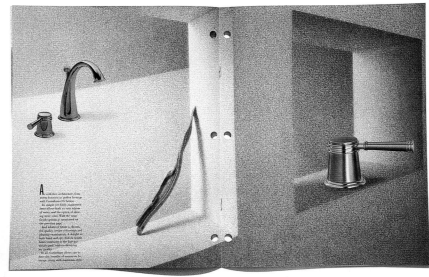

2

4

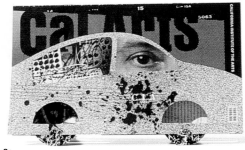

3

1. Promotional brochure with die-stamped objects which can be assembled, for Georgia Pacific, a paper manufacturer.
2. An interactive viewbook for California Institute of the Arts.
3. + 4. Brochure for Artistic Brass faucets.
5. Brochure on an edition of work by artist, Robert Rauschenberg for publisher, Gemini G.E.L.
6. Brochure highlighting the art and environment of South Coast Plaza, a shopping and business development.

5

6

COY, LOS ANGELES

9520 Jefferson Blvd.   Culver City, CA 90232   213/837-0173 FAX: 213/559-1706

1. Advertisement for textile manufacturer.

ATLANTA
JERRY
PAIR &
ASSOC.

BOSTON
LENI'S

CHICAGO
HOLLY
HUNT
LTD

DALLAS
DAVID
SUTHERLAND

DENVER
SHEARS &
WINDOW

HOUSTON
DAVID
SUTHERLAND

LAGUNA
NIGUEL
J. ROBERT
SCOTT

LOS
ANGELES
J. ROBERT
SCOTT

MIAMI
JERRY
PAIR &
ASSOC.

MINNEAPOLIS
HOLLY
HUNT
LTD

NEW
YORK
LUTEN
CLAREY
STERN

SAN
FRANCISCO
SHEARS &
WINDOW

SEATTLE
WAYNE
MARTIN

WASHINGTON
D.C.
THE
RIST
CORPORATION

J. ROBERT SCOTT

TEXTILES

The firm serves clients from all disciplines —finance, consumer products, energy, the arts, high technology and medicine, to name a few.

Whatever the area, Jim's favorite kind of client is one who "knows and understands the value of good design…one who interacts with us and becomes a part of the process."

The firm, operating out of Los Angeles and San Francisco, creates corporate communications, marketing communications, corporate identity and environmental graphics. "Our approach to design is an honest one," says Jim. "We're not driven by fads or trends, but by solid and intelligent communication."

Cross Associates is part of Siegel & Gale, a Saatchi and Saatchi design company. The Cross office is one of an international network of design firms.

"This larger network will give us more opportunity to work on international projects," says Jim.

1

Cross Associates   Designers

1. James Cross.
2. Self-promotion poster.
3. Annual report for Union Fed.
4. Annual review brochure for Capital Markets Group of Bank of America.
5. Symbol for a Japanese software manufacturer, Konami Industries Ltd.

2

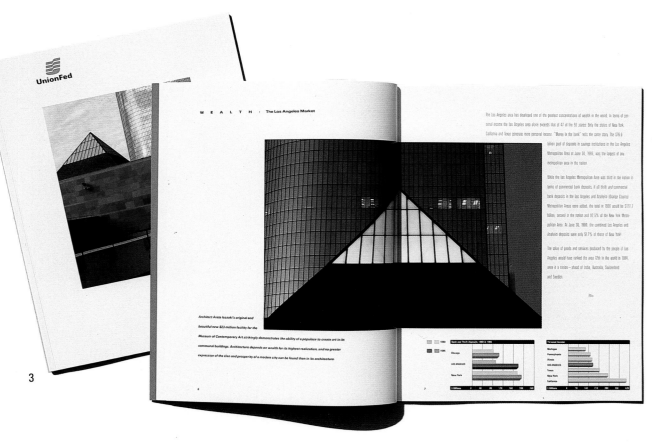

3

4

5

1. Symbol for Poetry Festival LA 87.
2. Peace poster for the Hiroshima Museum.
3.-7. Promotional material for Simpson Paper Company.
3. Reintroduction of a paper line with a new color palette.
4.+5. Pages from a brochure titled "Tools of the Trade."
6. Poster for coated papers.
7. Poster introducing a line of stationery papers.

POETRY
FESTIVAL
LA 87

1

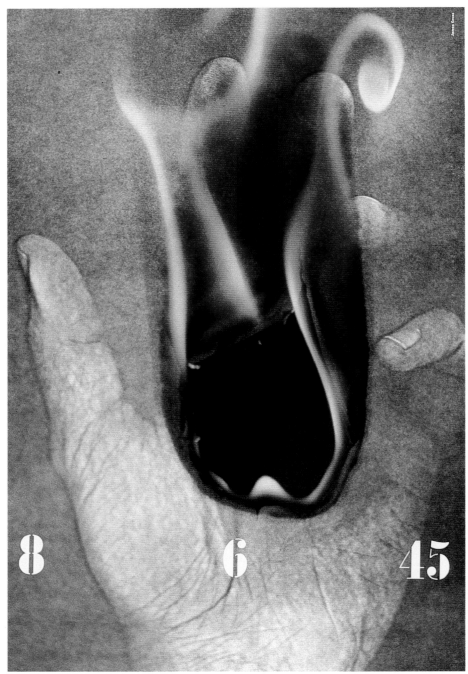

2

3

4

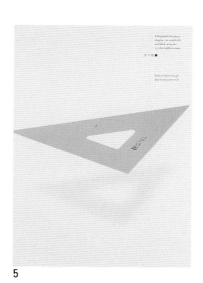

5

6

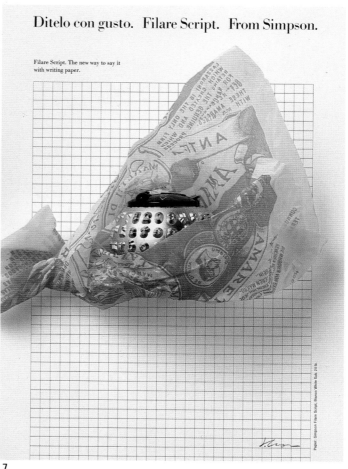

7

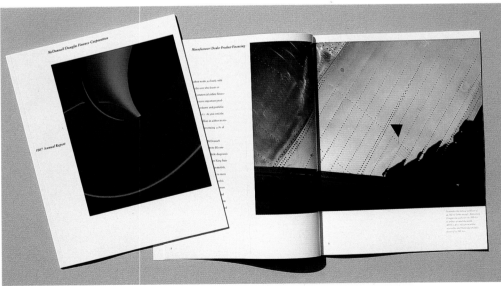

1. Bi-lingual brochure promoting the development of a Disney property in Europe.
2. Annual report for McDonnel Douglas Finance Corporation.
3. Signage, a 3-dimensional representation of the symbol for a fabric company.
4. Brochure series, announcing showroom openings for a furniture manufacturer.
5. Annual report for Measurex, a company which creates measuring devices for industry.
6. Recruitment brochure for an accounting firm.
7. Symbol for Bernards Bros., a construction firm.

1

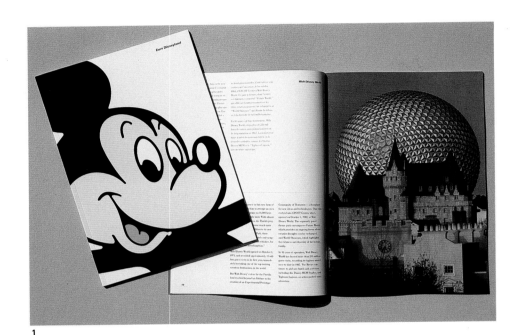

2

3

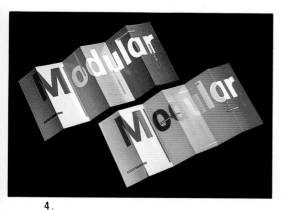

4.

5

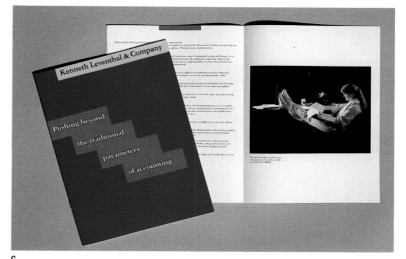

6

7.

CROSS ASSOCIATES

· ·

10513 W. Pico Blvd.   Los Angeles, CA 90064   213/474-1484 FAX: 213/474-4718

1

2

3

1. Call-for-Entries poster for American Institute of Graphic Arts.
2. Symbol for The Los Angeles Festival, a celebration of the performing arts.
3. Poster and catalog cover for U.C.L.A.

UCLA SUMMER SESSIONS 1986
Catalog available in March   Los Angeles, California 90024   213 825-8355

THE DESIGNORY, INC.

Working out of a sprawling Victorian home and the adjoining office complex, The Designory boasts a creative contingency of over 30 staff and in-house freelance designers, writers and illustrators. In addition, a complete typesetting and stat service is located on the premises.

Principals Dave Almquist and Steve Fuller have organized the Long Beach-based company as a full-service marketing and design source, placing emphasis on quality work and the effective management of major programs.

"We like to think of ourselves as an extension of our client's advertising agency. If our client spends over a hundred million on television and print, they shouldn't drop the ball at point-of-sale, in collateral, packaging or anywhere else the company's image is on the line."

While The Designory handles a group of accounts that range from motorcycle hardware to computer software, they have a special expertise in the automotive industry. In their 17-year history, they've produced over one thousand projects for automotive clients from Stuttgart to Japan. As Almquist says, "We love cars."

1.

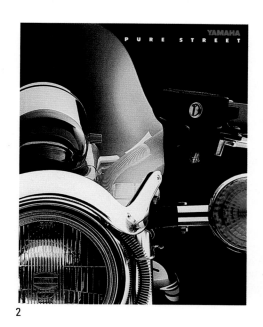

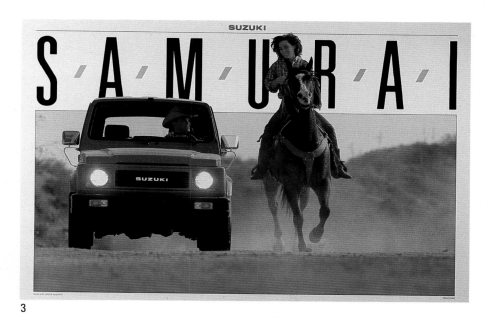

2

3

4

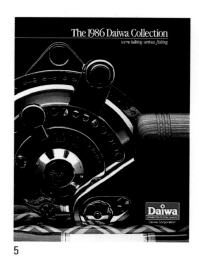

5

1. The Designory.
2. Catalog for motorcycle accessories.
3. Poster for Suzuki.
4. Gatefold cover for a Mercedes-Benz brochure.
5. Catalog for fishing equipment.

1.+2. Cover and spread for consumer brochure.
3. Part of a system of brochures.
4. Spread from brochure.
5. Dealer program for Suzuki.
6. Spread from consumer brochure for Samurai.
7. Scenes from a showroom video for Samurai.

1

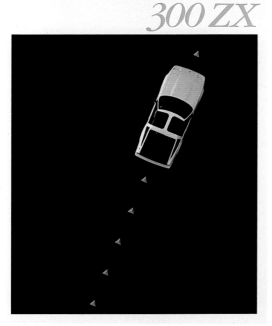

2

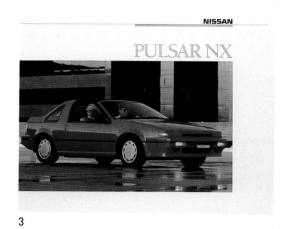

3

4

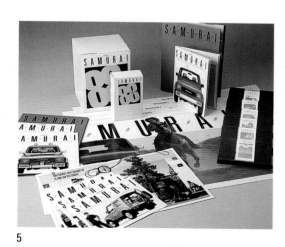

5

6

7

1. Dealer kit for Mercedes-Benz.
2. Dealer award for Mitsubishi.
3. Catalogs for Porsche.
4. Spread from boutique catalog.
5. Symbol from Precision Automotive Products.
6. Symbol for the Long Beach Marathon.
7. Symbol for Eastman Office Systems.

1

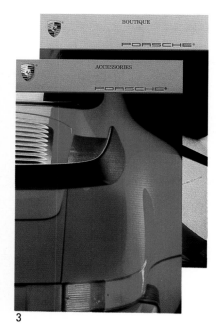

3

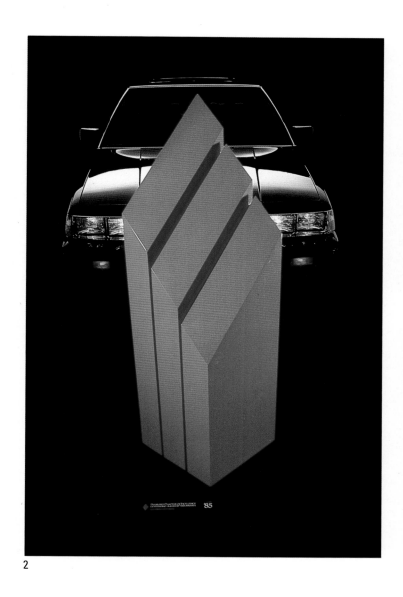

2

4

5

6

EASTMAN

7

2

1

3

4

5

1.+3. Annual report for the Port of Long Beach.
2. Catalog for marine equipment for Yamaha.
4. Trade advertisement for Sunkist.
5. Brochure for computer hardware for TEC America.

ROD DYER GROUP, INC.

If you ask someone in Rod Dyer's group for his or her business card, be prepared for something different.

Like a rooster. Or a cow. Or a sheep. Barnyard animals grace the group's own visual identity program. Partly because the firm is housed in a barn-like atmosphere. But mostly because it's different.

That's the way Rod Dyer likes things. "I'll hire an illustrator in London or a fashion photographer for a packaging program just to get a look that's unexpected," explains Dyer.

Specializing in the entertainment and corporate industry, the company is built around two divisions, print and video.

"Our designers are very well-rounded," the principal says. "Some of them direct our videos, some write their own copy." Whatever project the Dyer group is working on, they watch trends. And look toward setting new ones.

1

2

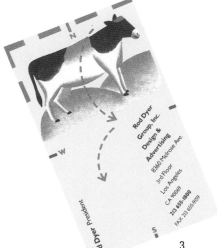

3

4

1. Film promotion poster for 20th Century Fox.
2. Film promotion poster for Atlantic Entertainment Group.
3. Part of the identity system for the studio.
4. Film promotion poster for Universal.
5. Theatrical poster for The Ahmanson Theatre, Los Angeles.

5

S·P·U·N·T·I·N·O

1

2

CINEFLEX PICTURES

3

4

THE DISNEY CHANNEL

5

6

7

8

9

1. Logotype for an Italian restaurant, San Francisco.

2. Monogram for MCA.

3. Symbol for a film production company.

4. Logotype for a television program.

5. Symbol for The Disney Channel.

6. Symbol for Eagle Records.

7. Logotype for an Italian restaurant, San Francisco.

8. Logotype for a hotel.

9. Symbol for an Italian restaurant, Los Angeles.

10. Packaging system for Croissants, USA.

11. Packaging system for Oublier, women's cosmetics.

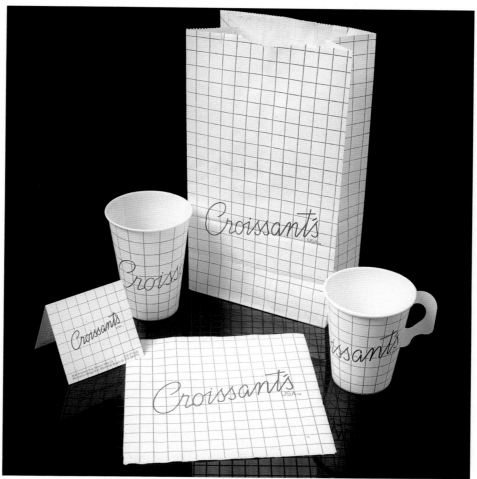

10

11

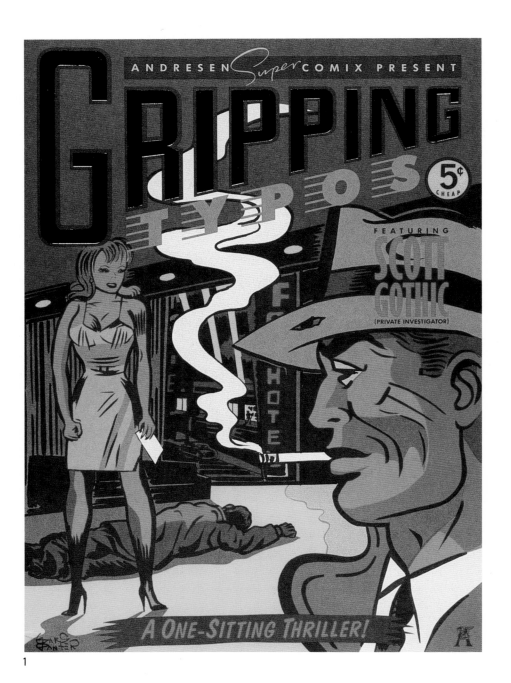

1

1. + 2. ''Gripping Typos'' a promotional brochure for Andresen Typographics.
3. Poster for Sagra del Vino, an Italian restaurant, Los Angeles.
4. Direct mail brochure for a retail shop.
5. Annual report for Jones Intercable, Inc.

3

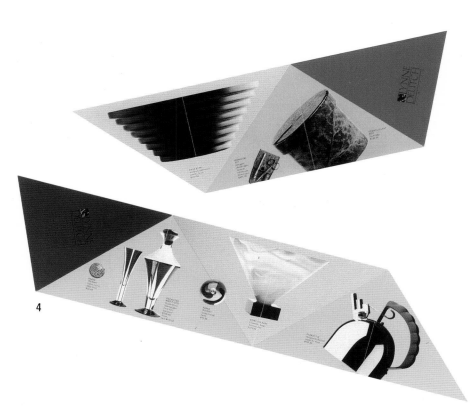

4

5

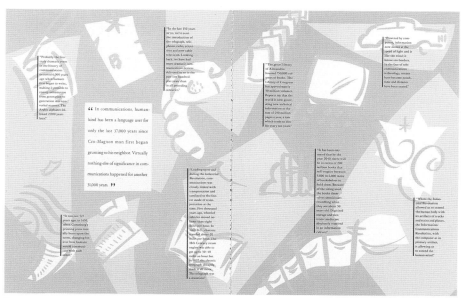

5

1

2

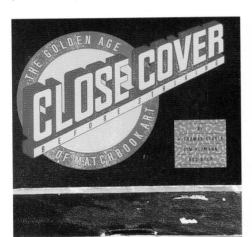

3

4

1.-5. Two hardcover special-interest books designed by the studio for Abbeville Press.

5

STAN EVENSON DESIGN INC.

"If a client says, 'We need a press kit,' a lot, of designers would think about what exists. We think about what we can create," says Stan Evenson.

Since 1976, Stan Evenson Design Inc. has operated with the goal of creating new and different solutions to help people. In that time, the group has handled a diverse project list—from corporate identity and collateral to packaging, advertising and signage.

Evenson feels a project is most successful when the client shares in the enthusiasm of the end result. "You have to have the ability to sell your work," he says. "But you also have to have the work to sell."

1

1. Stan Evenson, Barbara Hamagami, David Sapp, Shari Norwood and Peter Nomura.
2. Presskit, vacuum-formed for Honda.
3. Computer-generated artwork for a magazine cover for a real estate developer.
4. Packaging for men's cologne.

2

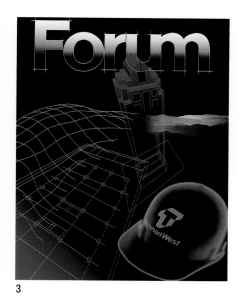

3

4

119

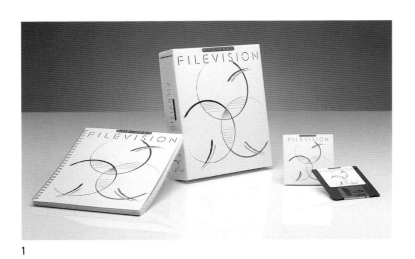

1

1. Packaging for software.
2. Pharmaceutical packaging.
3. Promotional poster for a jazz group.
4. Logotype for food exporters.
5. Symbol for Martha Productions, artists representatives.
6. Symbol for Mellinger Insurance Brokers.
7. Symbol for a record company.
8. Logotype for a photostat service.
9. Symbol for a record company.
10. Symbol for Force One, software design and manufacturer.
11. Logotype for a sparkling wine.
12. Symbol for First Rep, electronic parts sales company.

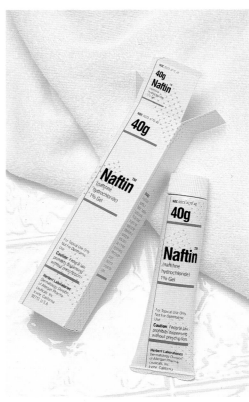

2

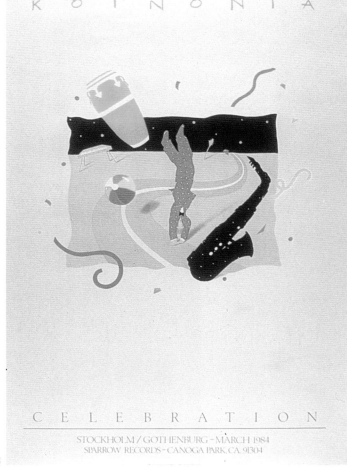

3

4

5

6

7

8

9

10

11

12

THE · ADVENTURES · OF
VLADIMIR · LANGE

1

IMAGES CAPTURED

Forty below zero. We were camped at 20,000 feet, but the windswept summit of Peak Lenin still loomed high above us. A frigid gust just blasted one of our tents off the ridge and into China.

Conditions at this altitude are harsh—mountaineers call it "the death zone." But there is nothing I enjoy more than bringing back images from locations that others consider impossible.

Photographing people is like climbing mountains: You don't conquer; you approach with understanding, and seek acceptance. I spent half of my life among the cultures of Europe, South America and the Middle East. In a California factory or in the dim yurt of a Kirghiz nomad—I am accepted, and I am welcome.

WELCOME

Everest veterans. Russian climbers in the Pamirs. Kirghiz SSR.

Descendants of the Incas at the Institute of the Cordillera Blanca, Peru.

Khumjun Festival—fashion show in beautiful down from Kathmandu, Nepal.

Mountaineer at sunrise in the Sierra Nevada, California.

2

Buchalter,
Nemer,
Fields
&
Younger

4

Buchalter,
Nemer,
Fields
&
Younger

CORPORATE

The Corporate group at Buchalter, Nemer, Fields & Younger is involved in business transactions of every kind. As general counsel and as special counsel for specific transactions, our attorneys group represent a wide range of closely-held and publicly-held businesses. The Corporate group provides advice and services for all legal aspects of business operations, including organization, capital formation, merger and consolidation, sale and acquisition of stock and assets, reorganization, recapitalization, liquidation and dissolution.

The Corporate group's experience and expertise encompasses a significant securities practice including all areas of federal and state securities laws. Our attorneys assist clients with structuring, negotiating and drafting corporate finance transactions. They regularly handle matters involving the Securities and Exchange Commission, regional and national exchanges and state securities authorities. The Corporate group often assists clients with the preparation of annual reports and proxy statements, as well as other reports filed with the Securities and Exchange Commission.

Our business practice also includes representation of new ventures, commencing either at formation or later stages of financing.

Our attorneys advise on a range of matters, including:

- formation of business entities, including corporations, general partnerships and limited partnerships

- public and private offering of securities of all types, such as equity and debt offerings, limited partnership offerings and exchanges
- periodic reporting and compliance with federal and state securities laws
- proxy solicitations and contests
- takeovers, mergers, acquisitions and divestitures
- leveraged buyouts
- shareholder agreements and shareholder dispute resolution
- a broad range of complex and routine contractual arrangements
- venture capital financing
- franchising and licensing
- international business transactions (licensing, distribution, joint ventures), as well as structuring of multinational companies including international tax aspects thereof
- formation of captive insurance companies, including offshore entities, and risk retention groups
- federal and local laws and rules regulating California campaign contributions

12

13

EXTERIOR 100% ACRYLIC HOUSE PAINT WATER BASE

GANAHL
SINCE 1884
CENTURY
· PAINTS ·
ORIGINAL

ONE GALLON
3.78 LITERS

WHITE & PASTEL BASE
2001

3

1.+2. Promotional brochure for a photographer.
3. Label design for custom paint.
4. Capabilities brochure for a law firm.
5. Packaging for an Australian diet soft drink.
6. Merchandising kit for Mattel.

5

6

1

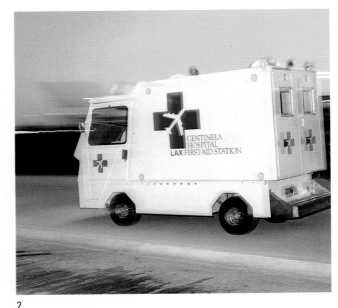

2

3

1. Identity and signage application for a franchise.
2. Symbol and signage for airport medical clinic.
3. Logotype and signage for a type and color house.
4. Promotion bag for trade show.

124

4

"The more good designers who come into the Los Angeles market, the better for all of us," believes John Follis. He knows that competition breeds the drive for excellence. And he approaches design with that goal in mind.

So does his son, Grant. Together they have established a design firm that inextricably links architecture and interiors with environmental and printed graphics. Since 1960, the company has attracted clients ranging from international corporations to growing communities in search of new identities.

The challenge for Grant is achieving an appropriate balance between a contemporary approach and classic interpretation. "Corporate identities, by nature, require a certain level of permanance, yet every design should create excitement. The best designs reside on the fine line between the two."

Both John and Grant Follis have an affinity for their area of expertise. They've built a company of designers who understand the difference between designing a brochure which may last for one year and designing a signage program or interiors project, which, one hopes, will last a generation.

1

2

3

4

5

1.-5. Signage system for Newport Center, Newport Beach, California.

1.-6. Signage system for California
Museum of Science and Industry,
Los Angeles, California.
4. Detail of entrance sign.
7.-9. Signage system for Roxbury Park,
includes directory, backboard and
park rules.

1

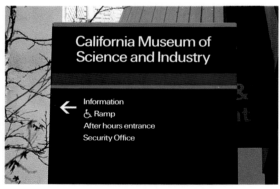

2

3

4

5

7

6

8

9

Downtown
MANHATTAN BEACH

1

2

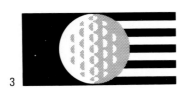

3

4

5

R

6

7

8

1. Symbol for the business district redevelopment project for the city of Manhattan Beach, California.
2. Leasing brochure for Greystone.
3. Symbol for American Golf Corporation.
4. Symbol for The Panda Inn restaurants.
5. Symbol for Griffin Development Company.
6. Proposed Symbol for Rancon Development Company.
7. Logotype for a restaurant in Los Angeles.
8. Symbol for San Antonio Health Services.
9.-11. Leasing brochure for a historical landmark renovation in association with Carlos Diniz Associates.

9

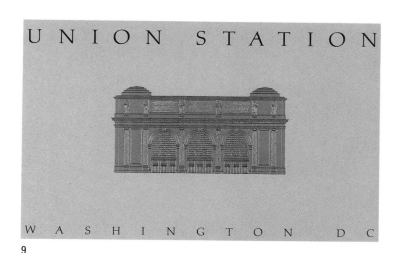

10

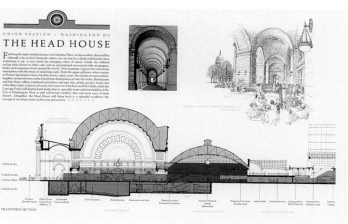

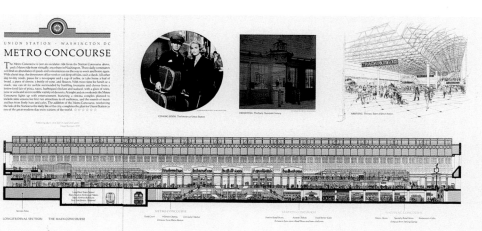

11

FOLLIS DESIGN

2124 Venice Blvd.   Los Angeles, CA 90006   213/735-1283 FAX: 213/730-1334

1

2

3

4

1. The J. Paul Getty Museum, Santa Monica, California.
2.-4. Signage system for The Getty Museum.
5.-6. Signage pylons at Northrop Plaza, Century City, California.

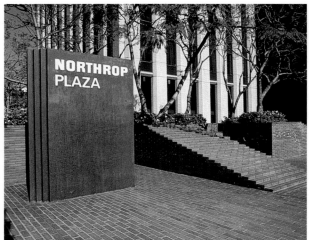

5

132   6

JOSH FREEMAN/ASSOCIATES

According to Josh Freeman, "Companies hire designers to achieve a marketing objective. Fortunately, good results and good design are almost inevitably two sides of the same coin." And in this company, results are the bottom line.

Freeman's group brings this approach to every project, whether creating a label for a wine bottle, or a cohesive system of marketing tools for a corporate client. "Every solution is market-driven," says Freeman. "We learn as much as we can about the target audiences, and the way a client's product or service meets their needs. And we establish very specific criteria. Only then do we take off and show what we can do."

What they can do is evident by the rows and rows of awards on the walls. As Freeman adds, "Awards are terrific, but so are satisfied clients."

1

JOSH FREEMAN / ASSOCIATES

3

1. Josh Freeman, Greg Clarke,
Vickie Sawyer, Trudy Bush, Catherine
Flynn and Nicki Freeman.
2. Part of the signage system for a
housing development in Venice, California. Signage features polychrome
plants and animals.
3. Logotype applied to banners.

2

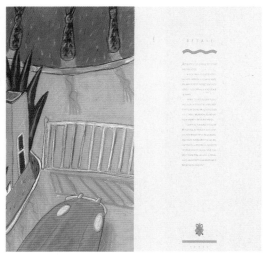

1

2

3

4

5

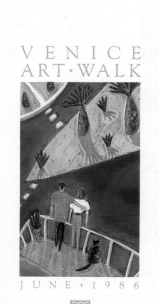

6

7

1. Move-in gift for new residents.
2.-4. Sales brochure featuring Karen Mercedes MacDonald's illustrations.
5. Promotional poster.
6. + 7. Advertisements for Del Rey Colony.
8. Call-for-Entries poster for the Olympic children's art contest sponsored by Levi-Strauss.
9. Entry monument for a group of single-family homes in Huntington Park, California.

8

9

1

2

1. Symbol for Fenton Partners, a residential real estate development firm.
2. Symbol for MedTec International, exporters of American medical technology.
3. Symbol for rare coin auctioneers.
4. Symbol for a recreation and dining club located in a group of three circular towers.
5. Symbol for AMI's Arthritis Center.
6. Symbol for a tennis tournament chaired by Monty Hall, host of the game show "Let's Make a Deal."
7. Commemorative poster honoring Los Angeles Times columnist.
8. Catalogue for the Craft and Folk Art Museum, Los Angeles.
9. Corporate capabilities brochure for Vedette Energy Corporation.
10. Poster for Shakespeare play on PBS.
11. Collection of educational materials for the mini-series "George Washington," sponsored by General Motors.

BOWERS AND RUDDY

3

MARINA
CITY CLUB

4

5

6

7

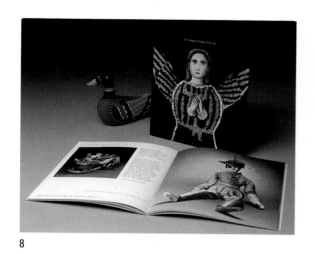

8

9

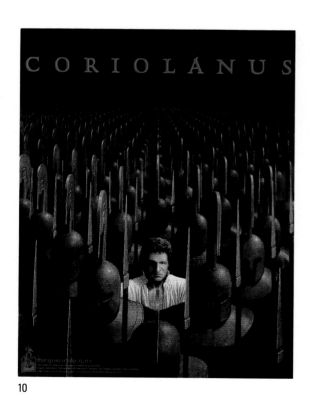

10

11

1

2

3

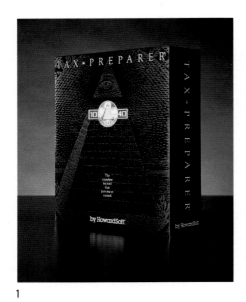

4

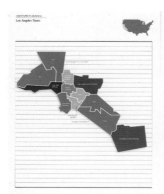

5

1. Packaging for Howard Software Services.
2.+3. Brochure for Grand Champions, a resort hotel near Palm Springs, California.
4.+5. Corporate fact book for the Times Mirror Company targeted to investment analysts.

140

Vahé Fattal and Russ Collins, a designer/ writer team, cofounded Fattal & Collins in 1982. Recently, they became affiliated with Grey Advertising.

"We began with the premise that we would only pursue projects that excited us," says Collins. "Consequently, our work covers the range from film posters to live action to motion graphics."

"Working in motion or live action is an interesting challenge because the added dimension brings a greater element of surprise. It's always new."

Vahé Fattal, who studied fine art at L'Ecole des Beaux-Arts in Paris, brings an impressive design background to the firm. "An assignment will typically have marketing goals and a long list of criteria, sometimes contradictory," he offers. "There's nothing more ineffective than a hybrid, unfocused solution, even if it addresses all the issues."

"The challenge for me, as a designer," continues Vahé, "is to find a solution that is beautiful in its simplicity, and perfectly clear in conveying the essential."

1

2

3

1. Vahé Fattal and Russ Collins.
2. Promotional poster for television mini-series.
3. Point-of-purchase system.
4. Promotional poster.

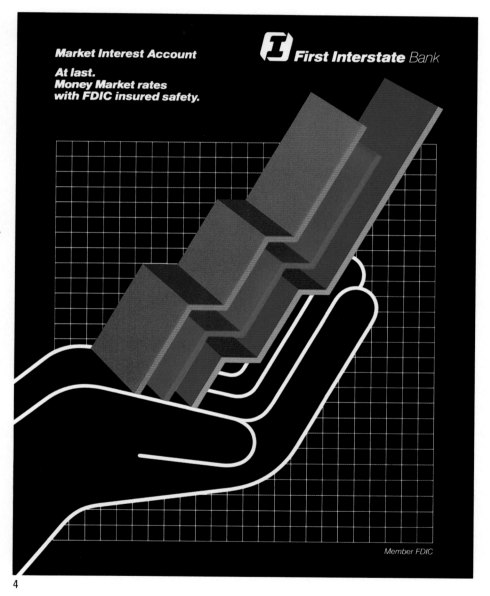

4

1. Logo design and theme/print application for ABC fall campaign.
2. Computer animated I.D. spot for ABC fall campaign.
3. Film title design.
4. Film title design.
5. Film title design.
6. Title design for a television series.
7. Title design for a television mini-series.
8. Title design for a television mini-series.
9. Symbol for a software company.
10. Symbol for a university's continuing education program.
11. Symbol for a film production company.

1

2

3

4

5

6

7

8

NELSON & BAUMAN

9

UCLA EXTENSION

10

ABC MOTION PICTURES

11

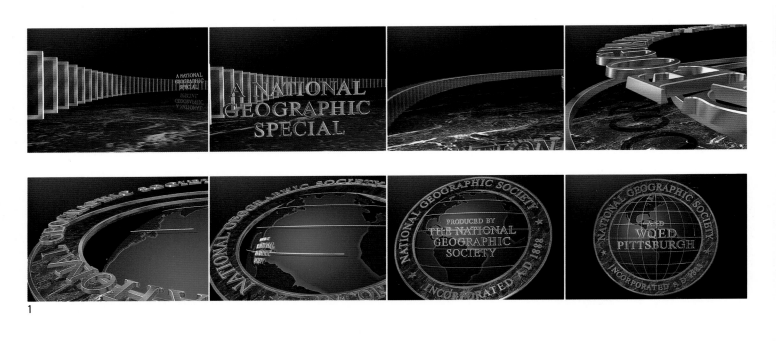

1

2

1. Computer-animated television show opener for National Geographic.
2. Computer-animated promotional graphics for ABC movies.
3. Promotional poster for continuing education art courses.
4. Proposed theatrical poster for a Broadway show.
5. Promotional poster for ABC Motion Pictures.
6. Promotional poster for United Artists.
7. Advertisement for a television mini-series.

4

3

5

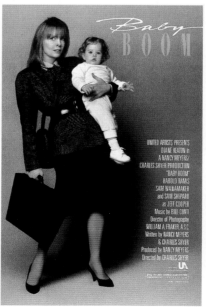

6

7

147

1

AMERIKA

2

1.+4. Identification spot for the mini-series "Amerika." Fifty individual spots were produced and played during commercial breaks.
2. Television mini-series title design.
3. Main and end titles for the mini-series.

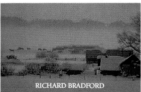

3

4

Gerry Rosentswieg started The Graphics Studio a little over twenty years ago with the idea that he never wanted to specialize in any one area of business. His award-winning work shows it.

Requests for poster design, packaging, brochures, annual reports, logo treatments and imaginative specialty items all share the project list at any given time, although the design group is probably best known for corporate identity programs. The idea is to keep moving, keep growing.

"Our staff of designers consists of generalists. We each take a different approach to the same problem," Rosentswieg says. Is that where the name The Graphics Studio—so obviously open-ended—comes from? Partly. But also, the principal smiles, "Nobody could spell Rosentswieg."

1

1. Gerry Rosentswieg
2. Studio interior
3. Museum poster
4. Calendar for The California/ International Arts Foundation.
5. Brochure for a hospital productivity consultant.
6. Symbol for an organization which creates and funds educational films relating to substance abuse.

2

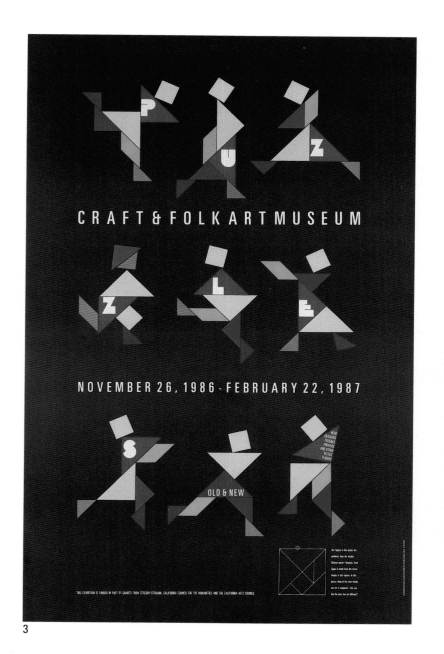

3

4

5

6

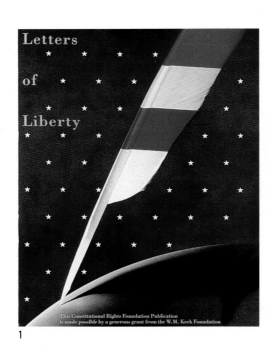

1

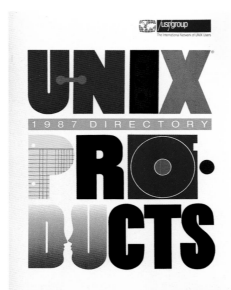

2

3

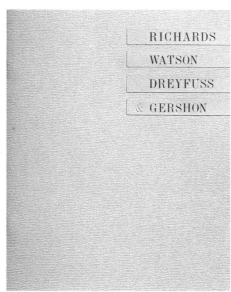

4

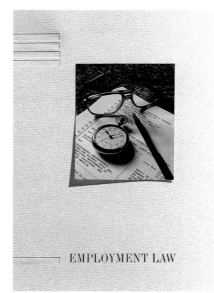

5

6

1. Book concerning the background of The Constitution, for use in secondary schools.
2. Directory of computer information.
3. Symbol for The A-Team, fine cabinetry fabricators.
4. + 5. Capabilities brochure for a law firm.
6. Logotype for a series of entertainment related companies.
7. Promotional packaging for The Los Angeles Philharmonic.
8. Magazine cover.

7

8

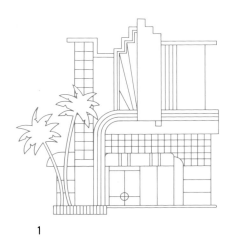

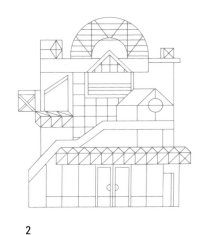

1.-6. Signature illustrations for shopping centers. From a series of more than forty for Schurgin Development Companies.
7.+8. Poster announcing the move of a development company. Detail shows open "A" with information about the move.
9. Poster for a convention.
10. Christmas packaging for a candy manufacturer.
11. Symbol for Turk Communications, Inc.

1

2

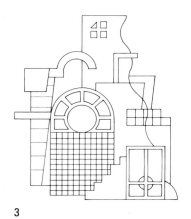

3

4

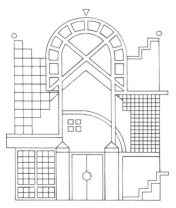

5

6

7

8

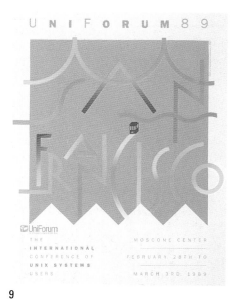

9

10

11

1

2

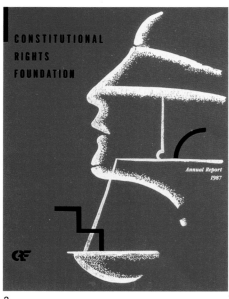

3

1. Part of the identity system and signage for a restaurant.
2. Membership brochure for The Craft and Folk Art Museum, Los Angeles.
3. Annual report for The Constitutional Rights Foundation.

In search of revolutionary design and ideas, April Greiman might draw on the latest computer technology as well as the oldest hand-set type. Most likely, both will find a place in the final product.

Over the last ten years, Greiman has pioneered Hybrid Imagery—the complex layering of elements to come up with a cohesive and appropriate design solution. This breakthrough approach is reflected in posters, videos, brochures, advertising campaigns, corporate identity programs and even sculptures.

"We're known for being innovative and experimental," says Greiman, "yet most of our work is applied to traditional problems and projects solved with sophisticated technology."

Bonnie Schiffman

1

Jayme Odgers

2

(di–zin´)

design april greiman inc

opening exhibition june 1987

we now have the exclusive for AKABA and Ingo Maurer.

2430 Main St .

Santa Monica

California

90405

213 392-9806

3

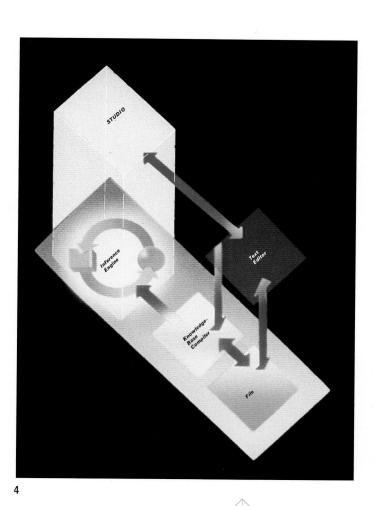

4

1. April Greiman.
2. China Club restaurant.
3. Advertisement for a furniture and object store.
4. Inference capabilities brochure "electronic diagram" illustrating an aspect of artificial intelligence.
5. Original Macintosh drawing for the diagram, designed by Eric Martin.
6. Packaging for Inference software.

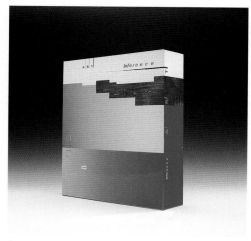

6

5

1

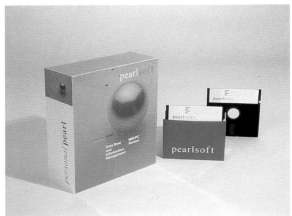

2

3

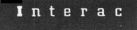

1. Presskit for interactive video corporation.
2. Packaging for personal computer software.
3. Brochure for a wind energy development corporation.
4. Shopping bag for men's clothing store.
5. Logotype for a framing and design objects store.
6. Sign for a florist in collaboration with Syndesis.

6

4

5

161

1

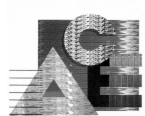

2

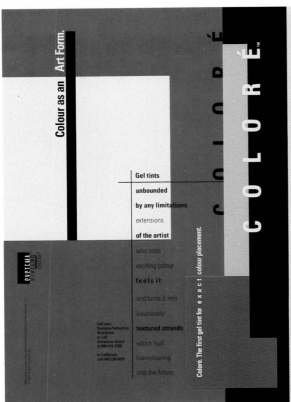

3

4

1. Advertisement illustrated and composed on the Quantel Graphic paintbox. Mannequin design: Robert Lobetta.

2. Symbol for Awards for Cable Excellence.

3. "Shaping the Future of Healthcare" composed with live video, the Macintosh computer, and the Quantel paintbox with assistance from Bob Engelsiepen.

4. Workspace poster composed with live video, the Macintosh computer, and the Quantel paintbox with assistance from Bob Engelsiepen.

5.-7. Poster and sculpture for Pacific Wave, for the Fortuny Museum, Italy. This poster and companion sculpture were composed utilizing the Macintosh computer. The sketches were then FAX'd to Italy where the sculpture and poster were manufactured. Assistant: Michael Ellison.

5

6

 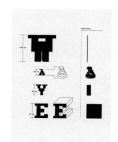  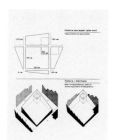 

7

APRIL GREIMAN, INC.

620 Moulton Ave., #211   Los Angeles, CA 90031   213/227-1222 FAX: 213/227-8651

1

1. Bookcover composed on the Graphic Paintbox at Electric Paint, Los Angeles.
2. Magazine cover for PC World. Outtake from the cover illustration. Composed with Macintosh computer and paintbox with assistance from Bob Engelsiepen.

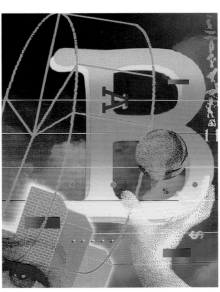

2

Since 1977, Christine Hershey and her staff have developed brochures, advertising campaigns, annual reports, corporate identity programs, point of purchase materials and packaging projects. "Basically," explains Hershey, "we get involved with anything that needs to communicate."

To better serve their clients, whose industries range from health care to entertainment, the firm has broadened their design services to include a unique, full-service marketing capability with the emphasis on results.

Headed by Hershey, Jeffrey Natkin, Director of Design and Dianne Endsley, Director of Marketing, the firm's goal is to consistently create innovative design and marketing solutions.

Throughout the Hershey organization runs a thread of high-charged enthusiasm. Hershey explains, "We really love what we do."

1

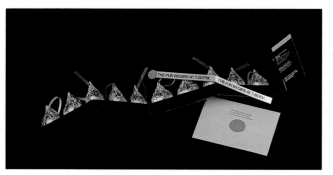

2

3

1. Jeffrey Natkin, R. Christine Hershey, Dianne M. Endsley.
2. Invitation for Hershey Associates ten year anniversary.
3. Hershey Associates building.
4. Call-for-Entries poster, Art Directors Club of Los Angeles.
5. + 6. Self-promotion brochure for the City of San Bernardino Economic Development Council.
7. Nursing recruitment brochure for the Hospital of the Good Samaritan.

4

5

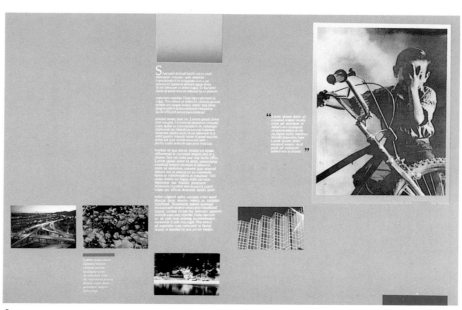

6

7

1

2

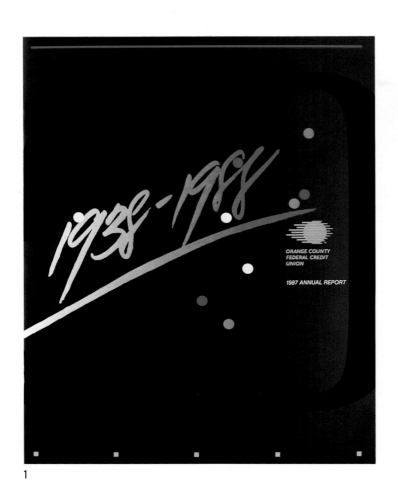

3

4

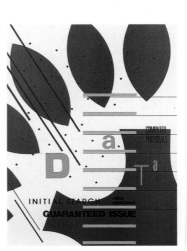

5

1. + 2. Annual report for the Orange County Federal Credit Union.
3.-5. Employee benefits posters for Corporate Financial Services.
6. Call-for-Entries poster for Bronze Quill competition for IABC.
7. Logotype for Artists for Peace exhibition.
8. Advertisement for Diamond Shamrock.
9. Brochure for Conceptual Instruments.

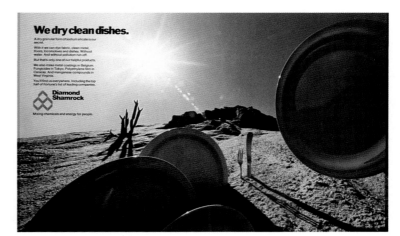

8

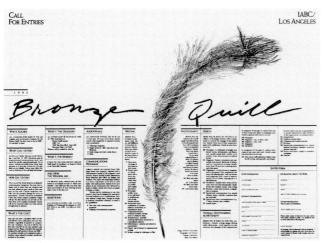

6

7

Aaron **Abrahams** Adams
Aguiar **Aguilera Ahlheim Ahmad**pour Aio**no Akens**
Alcala Alcantar Alcantara Alcoser Alejandro Alexan**der Allen**
Allrunner Allums Alonso Alonzo Alvarado Amador A**mezola Anaya**
Anderson Andrews Anguiano Antwane Appling Are**llano Armijo Armstead Armstrong** Aroonprapu
Arranaga Astorga Atkins Austin Avant Avila Ay**ala Ayers Barbarinde Babers Baca Badger Bailey Baker**
Ba**landran** **Bams B**anks Banuelos Barajas Barat**ta Barcenas Barnes Barnett Barney Barragan Barrera Barreto**
Barriga Baruch Bates Baughman Bautista Bayl**iss Baynes Beal Beamon Beaver Beebe Behanna Bell Bellows Benavides**
Benjamin Benson Berkley Bernal Bernard Berry Be**st Biddle Billops Bills Bird Black Blackwell Blaylock Blow Bolanos Bolton**
Bonbrake Bonner Bonnett Booker Bornstein Bradford **Bradshaw Bragg Braggs Branch Brandon Brantley Brazile Brewer Brewster**
Bridges **Briggs Briseno Brockington Brooks** **Broomfield Broussar**d Brown Brownridge Bruner Bryant **Bry**ce Buckner Bullard Bun Bunkley Burger Burghardt Burgos Burris Burson Butler
Byrd Caballero Cabrera Cain Calderon **Caldwell** Calhoun Callahui Calloway **Calnimptew Cambre Cam**field Canton Caporicci Carloss Carrillo Cars**on Carter Casas Casborn Castillo Castro Catano Cayode Ceballos Ceja Celestain** Celestine
Cephus Cerda Cerrano Cervantes **Chambers Cha**ndler Cha**s**e Chavarin Cherry Church **Cusners Claiborne Clark Clemo**ns Cleveland Cobarrubia Cobb Cody Colbe**rt Cole Coleman Collette Collins Conley Contreras Cook Cooks Cordero** Cordova Cortes Cortez
Courtney Covarrubia Cox **Craig Crawford** Crenah aw Cruz Cumbo Cunningham Curr ie **Curry Dag**nino **Daily Dandridge Dan**iel Daniels Darden Darosa Davidson Davil**a Davis Davison Daws Dean Deary Debois Del Cid Delatorre Delca**still Deleon Delong Demoss
Dent Desha Deville Diaz Dickinson **Dillon Dilvin**o **Dixon** **pOc**kery Doolittle Dorado Dottson **Dowdell Driscoll Dronyk Dubois** Ducksworth Duenas Duffey Dunlap Du**pr**ess Duran Durgan Earl Eaton Echevarria Edison Edwards Effin**g**er Eleby Elizalde Elliott Emanuel
Ennis Ephriam Escoto Esparza **Espinoza Esquivel** Estrada E**te**uati Etter Evans Faasisila Faison Faoa Farley **Farmer Favors Fears Felici**ano Fenderson Ferguson Figueroa Fishe**r Fix Flores Flournoy Flowers Floyd Foafoa Ford Fos**ter Franco Franklin Freeman French Frost
Fulbright Fuller Fultz Gainey **Gall**ard Garay **Garcia** Gardner Garlan**d Garrett** Garza Gaston **Gates** Gatlin Gaulding Geac oman Gee Gener George Gilford Gil**lon Gilmore** Gipson Givens Glaude Glenn God**don** Golden Gomez Gonzales Gonzalez Goodrich Gordon Goree Graham Grandberry Grant Gray Green Greene
Greenwood Gregory Grier Griffin **Griffins** Grigsby Grim Grundy **Guerrero** Guillory Gumms Guy Gu**z**man Haith Hall Ha**milton Hamlett** Hammler Handy Hankins Han sen Hanzy Harden Harmon Harper Harril Harris Har**rison Harston Hart Ha**rtford Hatzidakis Hawkins Hawley Hayes Haynes Haywood Hearon Hemphill
Henderson Hendricks **Hendrix** Herd Heredia Hernandez **Herron** Hicks Hid**a**lgo Hill **Hill**iard Hills Hilt Hi**nman** Hinshaw Hoard Hobbs Hodge Hodges Hodo Hoffman Holden Holiwell Holland Holley Holli**s** Holly House Howard Hudson Huff Huizar Hurtado Hyder Ibarra Imbruglia Ingram Ioelu Iose Isaacs Island Isrel
Jackson Jamison Javier Jefferies Jefferson Jenkins Jessop Jimenez Jobe Johnson Joll**a** Jones Jordan Ju**no K**akiva Kellum Kelly Kennedy Khalaf Kincad King Kinney Kirven Kitchen Knighten Knox Koonce **Ku**ria Lacy Lafitaga Lamothe Lane Larson Lattimore Lawson Lawton Leal Leatapo Leday Ledesma Leduff Lee Leggette
Leland Lemones Lemus Leos Lepe Lerma Lester Leverett Leyva Lic**On** Lincoln Lin**ton** Little Littlefie**l L**ivingston Locke Lockhart Logan Logologo I ondon Long Lopez Louden Louis Lovanh Lovato **Love Lowe** Loynaz Lozada Lucas Lucero Lu**j**an Luna Luster Lycans Lynons Machuca Macias Mack Madrigal
Magana Maglio Majid Maldonado Mammana Mann **Manuo** Marbury Marlow Marquez **Marshall** Martin Mar**tin**ez Masalosalo Mason Massey Matturi Maxwell May Mays McCall McClain McCloud McClure **McC**ollum **McCormick McCoy McCray** McDonald McEntarffe McFadden McGuire McHenry McKell McKennis
McKnight McLaurin McLendon McMillian Mc**Peters McRe**ynolds Meadows Medina **Me**dlock Meeks Me**jia** Melendez Mendez Mendoza Meza Miclat Mika Miles Millan Miller Mills **Miranda Mitchell Mock Monroe** Monroy Montemayor Montero Montgomery Montoya Moore
Moorehead Moosa Morales Morgan Mor**aica Morris** Mosley Mosqueda Mul**et Muniswamy Mun**iz Murdock Murphy Murray Murriel Naba Najar Nash Nation Naulls Nava**rre** Navarro Netterville Newborn Newman Niblett Nichols Nickerson Nickson Nieves Noda Noel Norman
Norris Nuno O'Connor Oden Oliver Olliso**n O'Neal** Ore**llano** Orozco O**rtiz** Osa Pacheco **Padilla** Parchman Parham Parker Parra Parrott Paschal Patino Patters**on Pa**yne Payton Paz Pedraza Pedroza Peeples Peinado Pele Pena Penate Perales Perdomo Perez Perkins
Perry Peters Petersen Peterson Pettigrew **Ph**elps Phillips Phipps Picado Pinedo Pitcher Pit**ts Pizzute** Plascencia Poarch Pollard Pompa Poole Porter Prado **Prince** Pritchett Prudhomme Purnell Qunder Quijas Quincy Quinones Quintero Quiroga Quiroz Radley Railey Ramey
Ramirez Ramos Randell Randolph Ransom Rayos Redix Reed Reeder Reese Reeves Regalado Register Re**n**gifo Renteria Reyes Ricart Richard Richards Richarson **Rich**mond Rico Rider Ridgeway Rieger Riggs Rios Rivas Rivera Rivero Rivers Roberts Robertson Robins Robinson Robles Rodgers
Rodriguez Rojas Romero Romes Rosales Rosas Rose Rosell Ross Rounds **R**ouse Ruiz Russell Rutherford Ryles Saavedra Sala**s Salazar Sald**ana Salelesi Sam Sampay Sampson Sanchez Sanders Sandoval Saucedo Scales Schnit**ger**
Schroder Scott Seaton Segura Sellers Sephus Sepulveda Serrano Sexton Shackelford Shallowhor Shanks Sharp Shephard Shipp Shogunle Shorter Sierra Silas Sillers Silva Simmons Simms Simpkins Sims Singleton Singtion
Skipwith Slaughter Sloan Smilden Smith Snell Solis Sparks Stacey Standmore Starcks Steen Stephens Stevens Stevenson Steward Stewart Stiger Stone Stoneham Sua Sullivan Summers Swisher Sykes Talley
Tatum Taylor Teofilo Tarrazas Terry Thomas Thompson Thornton Ticey Tigner Tilley Tillman Timmons Tisdale Tobar Torres Toscano Tran Travis Tremble Tibble Troupe Tryon Tse Turnbough
Turner Umana Urrea Useda Vaifanua Valdes Valdez Valdivia Valenzuela Valmore Vandyke Varela Vargas Vasquez Vaughn Vaultz Vazquez Veal Vega Velasco Venegas Venzant
Verdun Vernon Viamonte Vidaurre Villa Villagrana Villalba Villalobos Villegas Wahl Walker Wallace Ward **Warner Warren Washington Watkins Watson** Weaver Webb Wells
West Westfield Wheatley Wheaton White Whitestone Wiley Wilkerson Wilkinson Williams Williamson Willis Wilson Wimbish Winbush Wince Windley Wingate
Wingate Wingo Winston Wisner Witcher Witherspoon Wizel Wolfe Woodard Woods Wright Wynn Yealu Young Yracheta Zamora Zarate Zavala Zavalza Zayas Zuniga

1

2

3

4

5

1. Symbol for Saint Francis Hospital of Lynwood pediatrics department. "Baby Francis" is composed of the proper names of all the babies born at the hospital during their anniversary year.
2. Symbol for Interactive Financial Services.
3. Logotype for Jelly Bellies.
4. Symbol for National Association of Credit Unions.
5. Packaging for Maggio cheese.
6. Direct mail campaign for Commonwealth Bank.
7. Logotype for a real estate development.

6

7

HERSHEY ASSOCIATES

3429 Glendale Blvd.   Los Angeles, CA 90039   213/669-1001 FAX: 213/669-0613

1

1. Real estate brochure for First Development Corporation "101 Cheswald Lane."
2. Employee benefits package for Corporate Financial Services.

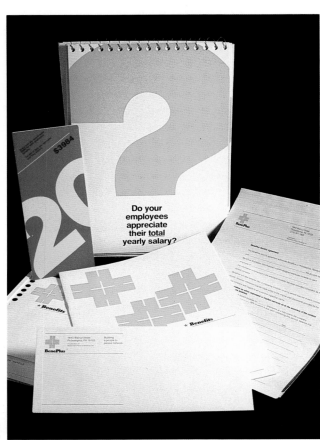

2

Three professionals, each with a different point of view—that's what Huerta Design offers its clients. Whether the project is a brochure design, packaging assignment or corporate identity program, this company has the expertise needed to come up with a solution.

In 1962, Hector and Carlos Huerta formed Huerta Design. A short time later, Octavio, the third brother, joined them. Since then, the firm has provided design services for a vast array of clients.

Their approach to business has grown out of first-hand knowledge: "Twenty-six years of communication experience has shaped a company philosophy that emphasizes creative design solutions to marketing problems."

1

2

3

4

5

1. Invitation to Huerta twentieth anniversary party.
2. Octavio, Hector and Carlos Huerta.
3. 25th anniversary invitation.
4. Brochure for Coldwell Banker.
5. Product brochure for Beckman.
6. Moving announcement.

6

1. Packaging for computer hardware.
2. Packaging for an optical company.
3. + 4. Packaging for garden
maintenance products.
5. Symbol for Indus Systems, a
computer peripheral manufacturer.
6. + 8. Packaging for imported wine.
7. Packaging program for a toy
manufacturer.

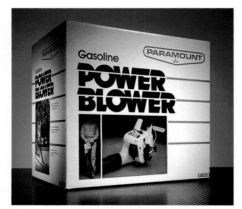

1

2

3

4

5

6

7

8

1

2

1. Self-promotional New Year's posters for the studio.
2. Capabilities brochure for Theodore Barry & Associates, management consultants.
3. Capabilities brochure for an agricultural company.
4. Symbol for Manualoha, a Hawaiian land development company.
5. Annual report for El Camino Resources, a computer leasing company.
6. Real Estate brochure for Coldwell Banker.

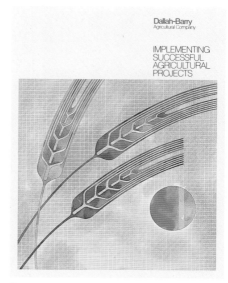

3

4

5

6

1

1.-3. Packaging design
Tyco Toys, Inc.

2

Tucked away in old town Pasadena, Wayne Hunt feels he has the best of both worlds. His design firm is freeway-close to Los Angeles, yet he and his employees enjoy a small-town atmosphere L.A. definitely doesn't offer. The firm, founded in 1977, moved to Pasadena five years ago.

"This town as a whole is rich in architectural heritage and environmental sensitivity," Hunt says. And that's important to him. Most of his clients revolve around the building industry—architects, land developers, interior designers and contract furniture makers.

The firm handles each step in the design scheme, from visual identity programs, architectural signing and graphics, product brochures and exhibit design, to specialty pieces that announce events. "I'm personally interested in the way graphic design translates into three-dimensional," Hunt offers.

Whatever the project, Hunt's approach to design is the same: "I believe in simple, clean work that communicates quickly. A design should offer something to the split-second viewer as well as to the committed reader."

1. Corporate identity manual for Union Federal.
2. Catalog for a furniture manufacturer, Kasparians.
3. Invitation to a showroom opening.
4. Advertisement, for Kasparians.
5. Press kit for Kasparians.

1

2

4

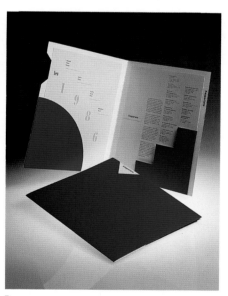

5

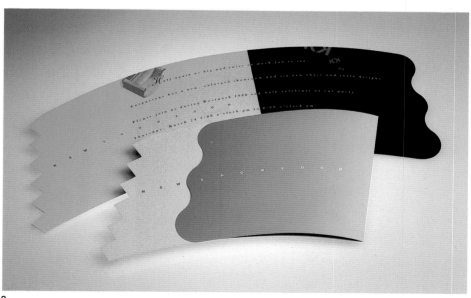

3

1

2

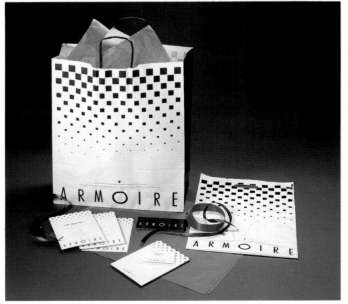

3

4

1. Packaging for Jonathans Cookies.
2. Logotype and stationery application for a custom monogramming company.
3. Poster for the City of Pasadena, Cultural Heritage Commission.
4. Packaging system for a sportswear boutique.
5. Symbol for The Los Angeles Philharmonic.
6. Symbol for The Architectural Foundation of Los Angeles.
7. Symbol for The Hollywood Bowl.
8. Symbol for Stephen C. Cannell Productions, a television production company.
9. Symbol for Stepping Stones, a tutoring company.
10. Logotype for Novita Clock Company.
11. Logo for Archiplan.
12. Symbol for The Drain Surgeon, a plumbing company.

LOS ANGELES PHILHARMONIC

5

6

7

8

9

10

11

12

2

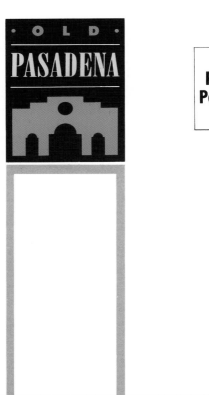

1

3

4

5

6

7

8

1.+2. Signage system for Old Pasadena, a redevelopment project.
3.-8. Signage system and graphics for California Plaza.
9. Monument sign showing dimensional version of symbol.

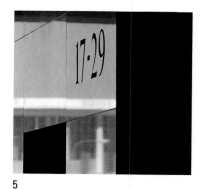

9

1

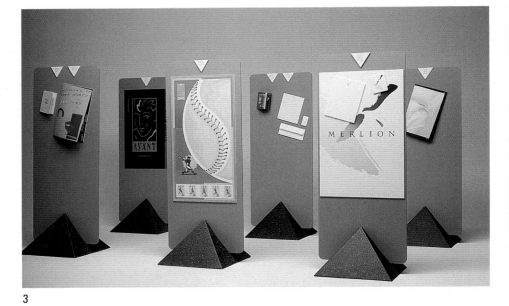

3

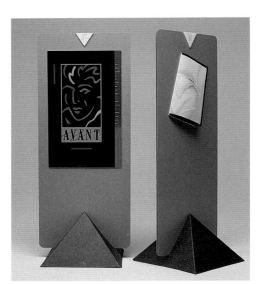

2

4

5

1. Spresso chair, designed for Kasparians.
2. Clock design, for Novita Clock Co.
3.-5. Modular exhibit design system for Simpson Paper Co.

INTRALINK FILM GRAPHIC DESIGN

Style first. That's the Intralink approach whether it's reflected in the design of their company headquarters or a pet project designed to save animals.

Primarily known for their expertise in the marketing of motion pictures, Intralink designs film and print promotional campaigns, as well as corporate identity programs, packaging and other merchandising tools for non-entertainment clients.

Principal Anthony Goldschmidt believes, "You have to assume the client is as good at what they do as you are at what you do. We ask a client to have the courage to let us do our best work—as much courage as it took for them to come out with their product."

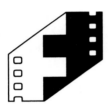

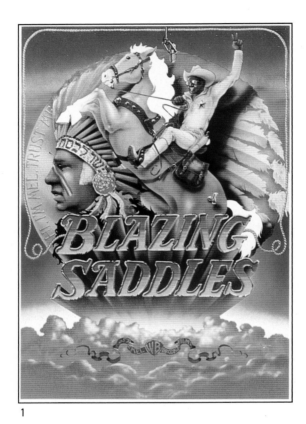

1

2

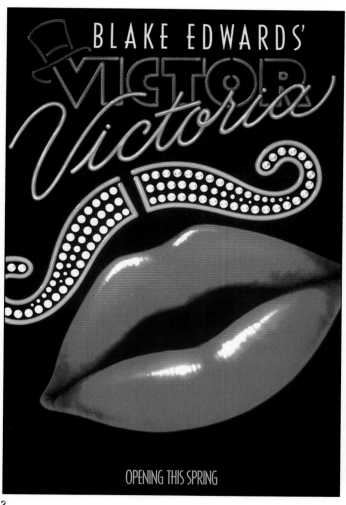

3

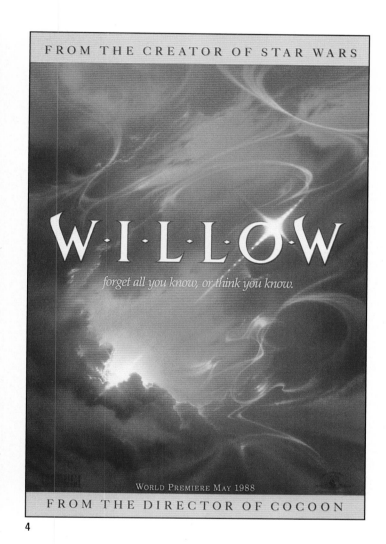

4

1. Warner Bros.
2. Los Angeles International Film Exposition (Filmex).
3. MGM/United Artists.
4. MGM/United Artists.

1. MCA/Universal Pictures, Inc.
2.+3. Public service poster and logo for The Cassidy Foundation.
4. MCA/Universal Pictures, Inc.

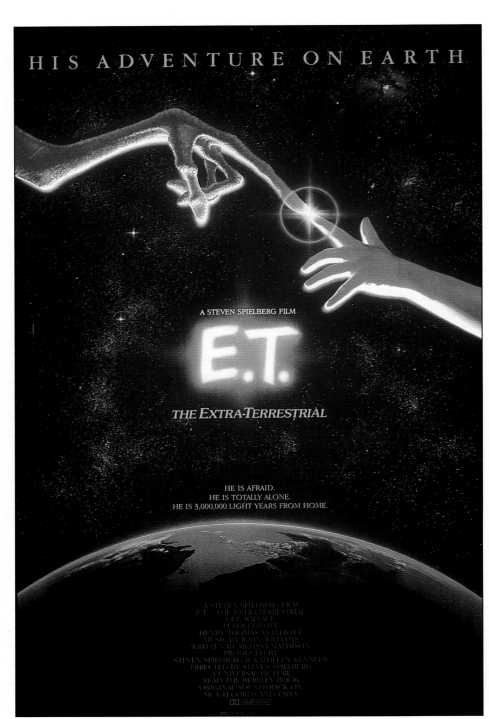

1

2

3

4

1. Tri-Star Pictures.
2. Logotype for bottled water.
3. Symbol for motion picture production company.
4. Logotype for Senator Tim Wirth, Democrat, Colorado.
5. Symbol for the largest realtor in Southern California.
6. Symbol for an auto racing team.
7. Symbol for an ocean front real estate development.
8. Logotype for an entertainment group.
9. Monogram for a product line.
10. Symbol for an entertainment group.
11. Logotype for an entertainment group.

2

THE LADD COMPANY

3

4

Realtors

JON DOUGLAS
COMPANY

5

CONDOR
RACING

6

7

CASTLE ROCK
ENTERTAINMENT

8

MAGNETIC VIDEO
A TWENTIETH CENTURY-FOX COMPANY

9

GLADDEN
ENTERTAINMENT
CORPORATION

10

BLAKE ENTERTAINMENT EDWARDS

11

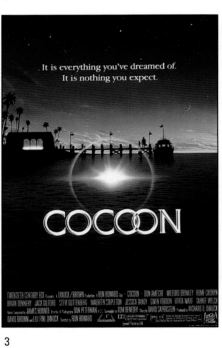

1

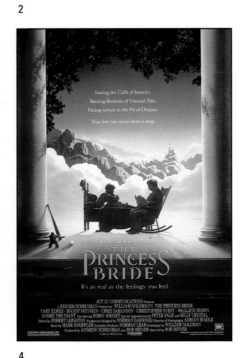

2

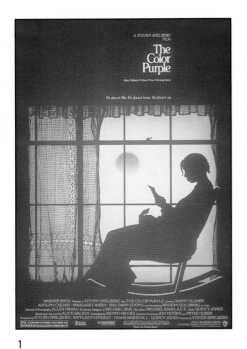

3

4

1. Warner Bros.
2. Warner Bros.
3. Twentieth Century Fox.
4. Twentieth Century Fox.

Founded in 1978, The Jefferies Association creates annual reports, corporate identity programs, collateral pieces, capabilities brochures, calendars, magazines and an occasional coffee table book.

Ron and Claudia Jefferies operate the firm from a renovated Dutch Colonial house near downtown Los Angeles, in an environment which is a combination of turn-of-the-century architecture and modern, custom-designed furnishings.

Of the Association's approach to business, Ron says, "We're the architects of a project, the managing partners, from concept to finish. As designers, we depend on the client's input. Working a problem out together has led to many creative breakthroughs."

1

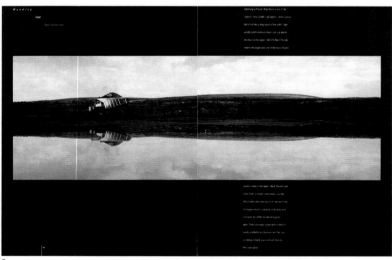

2

1. + 2. Annual report for ARCO.
3. + 4. Annual report for Fluor.
5. + 6. Annual report for Young People,
for The Signal Companies, Inc.

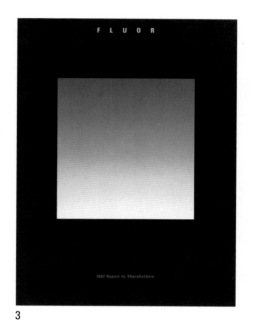

3

4

5

6

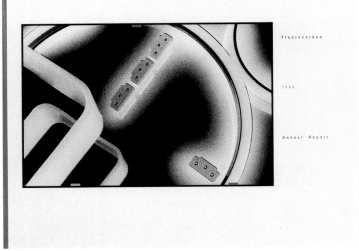

1

1. Annual report for Fluor.
2. + 3. Annual report for Fluorocarbon.
4. + 5. Annual report for Fluorocarbon.

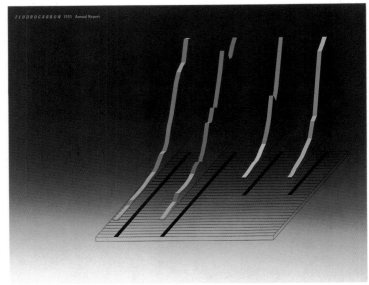

4

Fluid Sealing Group

All in all, 1986 was not an easy year. The group had its share of ups and downs and wound up the year under forecast in both sales and profits. Increased sales activity simply did not bring in as many orders as we had anticipated.

Fortunately, there were bright spots. In particular, nuclear O-ring orders and shipments continued strong. We've also seen solid growth in aerospace and defense, particularly the aircraft gas turbine market. And even though the petrochemical industry suffered terribly during the year, we were able to maintain good sales.

The rough spots included our oil patch related business. It followed the market, which was triple bad. Also, in the hydraulics and pneumatics market there was particularly heavy competition, which caused us to change our manufacturing and sales programs to respond to the shifting market conditions.

Well, what's ahead for 1987? Things are looking better, due in part to groundwork laid in the last half of 1986. Market plans and increased sales coverage which have been implemented should have favorable impact on at least four of Fluid Sealing's six divisions. Further, weakened dollars should help all divisions, except possibly Belgium. However, due to strong overall growth potential in Europe, we feel that Belgium will continue to prosper despite the strength of European currencies.

Looking at market categories, we see an upturn in the basic industries that looks good for all our divisions. Highlights here are increasing strength in the smokestack industries, and our belief that petrochemical and oil patch have bottomed out and should show some slight recovery during the course of 1987.

Aerospace and defense are expected to continue their growth, which will have positive effects on the Mechanical Seal, Components and Belgium Divisions. Increased activity in the space program as well as the renewed shuttle activity will give a boost to the Mechanical Seal Division. And as a group, we will show improvement in aircraft hydraulics due to new plans and products.

Major Markets

1986		1987	
30%	Petrochemical Fluid Handling	29%	Hydraulic & Pneumatic OEM's
25%	Hydraulic & Pneumatic OEM's	25%	Petrochemical Fluid Handling
18%	Aerospace & Defense	20%	Aerospace & Defense
6%	Specialty Machinery	7%	Specialty Machinery
5%	Medical & Scientific Instruments	6%	Medical & Scientific Instruments

Enover Division's Permanoid piston rings are used on this off-road dump truck's telescopic lift cylinders. The rings withstand an abrasive environment and offer reduced maintenance with a long wear-life.

Road graders are in constant daily use. Maintaining them is vital to continued operation. Universal Seal Division has a replacement kit for O-ring commonly used in the pivoting and turning front wheels. Oaking provides positive sealing and reduced maintenance.

Seals used on the engines and accessories of this executive jet are manufactured by the Mechanical Seal Division. Because of low friction operation and the ability to perform in high temperatures the Teflex spring seals are a must.

ten - eleven

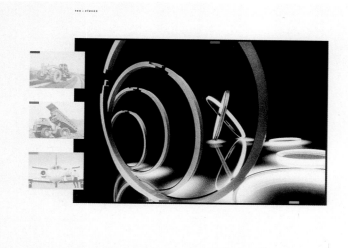

The Fluorocarbon Company

3

RUBBER GROUP

MAJOR MARKETS

23%	AUTOMOTIVE
22%	CONSTRUCTION
15%	OIL TOOL
11%	VALVE
6%	MEDICAL

We would like to be more upbeat about the rubber group markets but at this point we can't. The good news is that the largest market segment, automotive at 23%, shows the most promise for this year. So does medical, the smallest, 6% of the group's business. The valve business is mixed but it will continue to be a significant contributor. One of the off markets is oil tool and it will stay off all year, so its percentage of total group sales is bound to drop. Construction, 22% of our rubber volume, is starting slowly but should recover as the year progresses. It is going to be a challenge to maintain growth in the group this year.

four

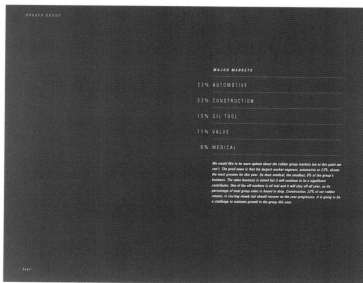

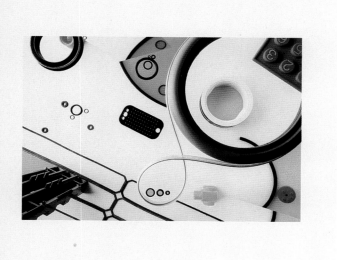

5

1

1.+2. Annual report for Baker Hughes, Incorporated.
3. Spread from a prior annual report for Baker Hughes, Incorporated.
4. Annual report for First City Industries, Inc.
5.+6. Annual report for Security Pacific Corporation.

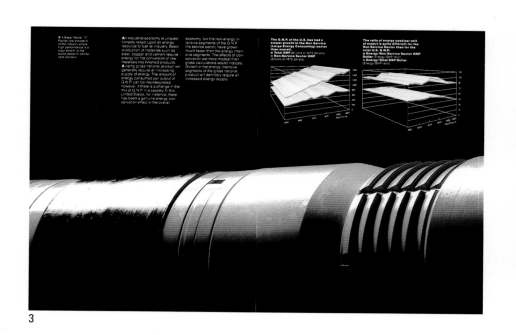

3

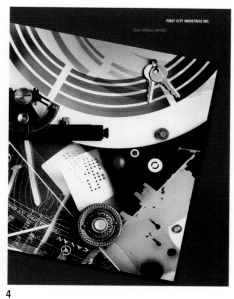

4

SECURITY
PACIFIC
CORPORATION

PERSPECTIVES

Annual
Report
1985

5

6

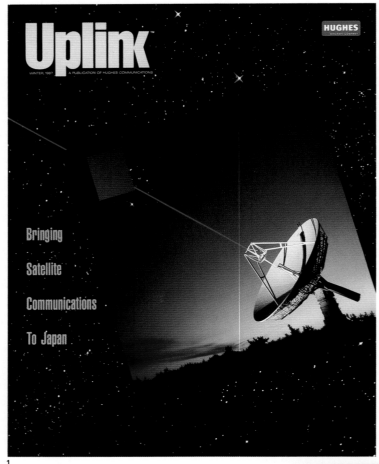

1

1.+2. Publication design for Hughes Communications.

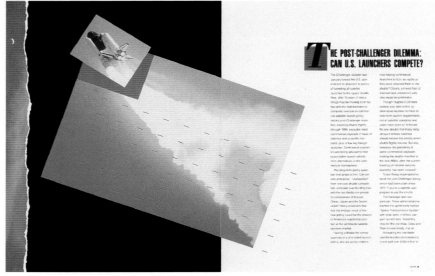

2

RUSTY KAY & ASSOCIATES, INC.

Rusty Kay likes motorcycles. That's the first thing you notice when you walk into his Santa Monica studio. Beautifully restored, gleaming motorcycles and bicycles—of all variety of vintages—drip from the ceiling.

For thirteen years, Rusty Kay and Associates has provided marketing consultation and communications tools to clients in every industry from automotive to technical to consumer. A common element in most of his client relationships is that they're long-standing. "I have major clients who have been with me since the beginning," Rusty explains.

The firm creates identity programs, annual reports, advertising, brochures, collateral pieces, packaging and posters. Whatever the marketing vehicle, Rusty Kay likes innovation. For his company. And his clients.

1

2

3

1. Lobby interior.
2. Rusty Kay.
3. Self-promotional poster featuring a 3-wheel Morgan from The Rusty Kay Collection.
4. Dealer sales materials for General Warranty Corporation, nation's leading automotive service contract company.
5. + 6. Product brochure for Rollcut Rotary Dies.

4

RollCut
Rotary
Dies

5

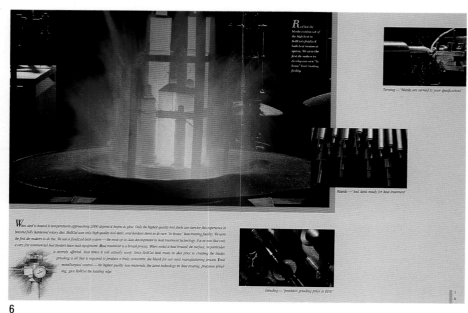

6

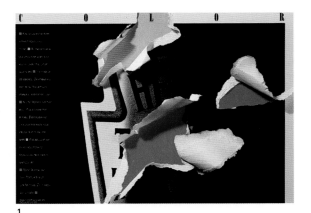

1

1. Poster for a color house.
2. Annual report for Casablanca Industries Inc.
3. Series of product brochures for Integrated Services Digital Network, a division of GTE.
4. Corporate capabilities brochure for Transpacific Development Corporation and project brochures for selected projects.
5. Stationery system for a color separator.

2

3

4

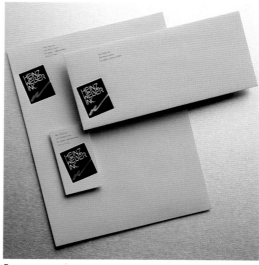

5

1

2

LIFE

3

ELDON
INDUSTRIES≈INC.

4

TANTOO

5

DUFF MEDAVOY INC.

6

7

MD BUYLINE

8

TOTALLY ♥ CHOCOLATE

9

10

11

1. Logotype for a color separator.
2. Symbol for Pegasus Realty, commercial real estate developer.
3. Symbol for a charity, "Love is Feeding Everyone."
4. Logotype for Eldon Industries, Inc.
5. Symbol for a company which manufactures suntanning decals.
6. Symbol for celebrity endorsement agency.
7. Logotype for an ink manufacturing company.
8. Symbol for a medical consulting service.
9. Logotype for a custom confectioner.
10. Corporate ID system for a medical consulting service.
11. Poster created for the favorite restaurant of Rusty Kay.

1. Identity system for a custom confectioner.
2. Packaging for a cable TV system.
3. Self-promotional Christmas packaging.

"The space a person works in is a prime influence on the ability to create," says Joan Libera. Her offices were designed for designers.

It's the space from which her staff creates annual reports, corporate identity, collateral programs, packaging, videos and audio/visual projects. For a whole array of clients, including real estate, financial, health care and entertainment.

Of her philosophy of design, Joan says, "We approach graphic design as a fine art, creating a concept for each specific project. We don't believe in a system of solutions. We analyze the problem."

1

3

2

1. Joan Libera
2. Studio interior.
3. The studio exterior.
4.+5. Annual report for Kaufman and Broad, Inc., an international housing and life insurance company.
6.+7. Annual report for Datron Systems, Inc.

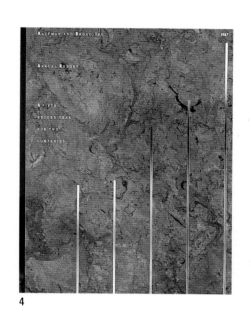

4

5

6

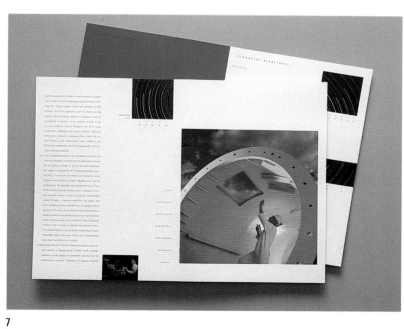

7

2

1

3

4

5

6

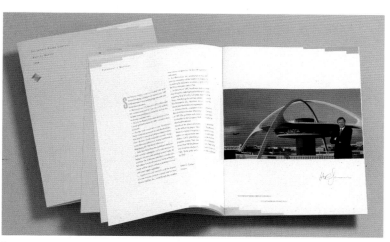

7

1.- 4. Annual reports for Aaron Spelling
Productions, Inc.
5. + 6. Brochure and leasing materials
for a real estate development.
7. Annual report for Southwest Water
Company.

2

1

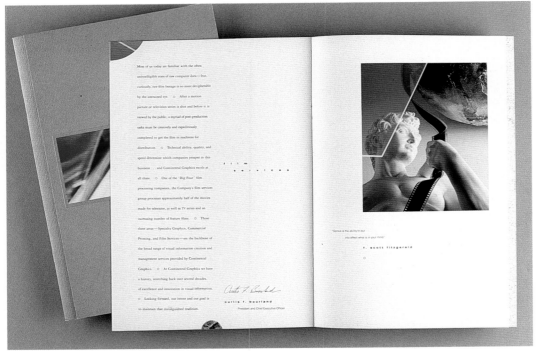

3

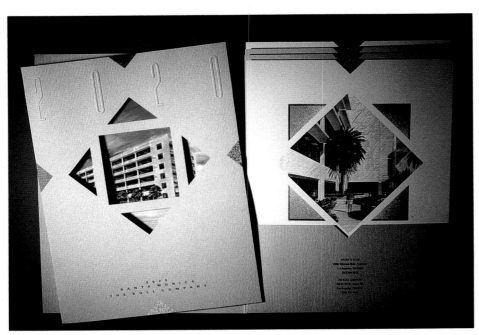

4

1.- 3. Marketing brochure for
Continental Graphics Corporation.
4. Leasing brochure for an office
building.
5. Symbol for an office building.
6. Logotype for The Art Directors Club
of Los Angeles.
7. Logotype for Western Health Plan.
8. Symbol for Southwest Water
Company.
9. Symbol for Precision Aerotech, Inc.
10. Logotype for a classical music line.

THE NEW

WILSHIRE

5

6

7

8

9

10

12020 W. Pico Blvd.   Los Angeles, CA 90064   213/477-2027 FAX: 213/477-9392

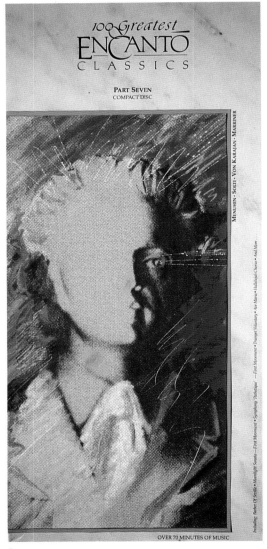

1

2

3

1.+2. Packaging series for
JCI & Associated Labels.
3. Video packaging for J.C.I. video.

"The graphic solution to a marketing problem should not simply be a creative impulse reflecting the mind of the designer," says Scott Mednick. "It is a reasoning process that takes all of the criteria into consideration."

Scott Mednick and his design staff apply that philosophy to all their projects, from corporate identity programs to package design to annual reports.

Scott maintains there are two rules to making each design individual and distinct. "Be creative," he advises. "And be appropriate."

1

2

3

UNCOMMON PLACE

WEST HOLLYWOOD
THE CREATIVE CITY

4

THE PLACE IS COOKIN'

WEST HOLLYWOOD
THE CREATIVE CITY

5

GO OFF YOUR ROCKER

WEST HOLLYWOOD
THE CREATIVE CITY

6

NO WEAR LIKE IT

WEST HOLLYWOOD
THE CREATIVE CITY

7

1. + **2.** Studio interiors.
3. Banners for the City of West Hollywood.
4. - **7.** Posters highlighting the creative industries within the city.

2

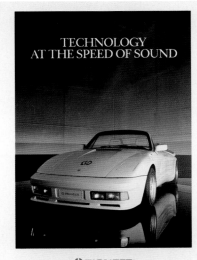

1. Packaging and collateral system for a line of imported scarves.
2. Symbol for Suzuki promoting snowboarding.
3. Promotional poster for Pioneer Car Stereo.
4.-6. Brochure for a film highlighting the film's production and stars.
7.-9. Capabilities brochure for a printer featuring a portfolio of their printed work.

TECHNOLOGY
AT THE SPEED OF SOUND

PIONEER
US TOUR 88

4

5

6

7

8

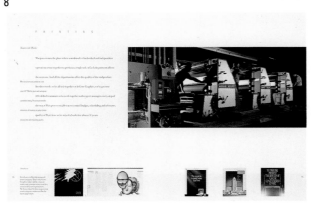

9

1

2

1.+2. Symbol, packaging and promotional materials for a bakery chain.
3. Packaging and product design for a board game.
4. Symbol for Balboa Development Group.
5. Symbol for Warren Eljenholm Consultants.
6. Symbol for Cinetex.
7. Symbol for Apex Video.
8. Symbol for Resnick-Steier, a real estate development company.
9. Symbol for Hi-Tops Video, a publisher of children's video.
10. Symbol for Prefam, who redesign urban centers.
11. Symbol for Primary Development Corporation.
12. Symbol for Vestron, Inc.

3

4

5

6

7

8

9

10

11

12

SCOTT MEDNICK & ASSOCIATES

7412 Beverly Blvd.   Los Angeles, CA 90036   213/938-3839 FAX: 213/938-8950

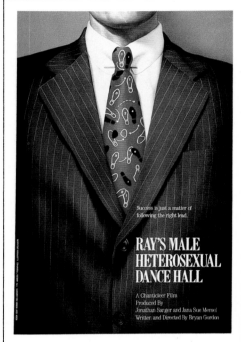

1. Promotional poster for the Samuel
Goldwyn Company.
2. Promotional poster for Chanticlair
Films.
3. Logotype for a motion picture.

MORAVA & OLIVER DESIGN OFFICE

Emmett Morava and Douglas Oliver love doing annual reports. "There's a real necessity for design authorship," comments Oliver. "Not only that, there's instant gratification. In three or four months, you can have a finished project you're really proud of."

The principles and senior designer Jane Kobayashi-Ritch are committed to doing all the actual design work themselves, with the assistance of a veteran production team. "When we talk to a client, they're talking to the people who will really do the work," explains Morava.

Both partners own impressive track records in annual report design, and their approach is one they both agree on. "We look at every aspect of the client's business, its strengths as well as its weaknesses," says Oliver. "In order to help them, we get to know them very well."

It pays off. As Oliver says, "Our clients become good friends."

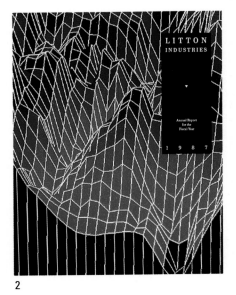

2

1

1. Emmett Morava, Doug Oliver and Jane Kobayashi-Ritch.
2. Annual report for Litton Industries.
3. Promotional brochure for a paper company.
4. + 5. Annual report for Pacific Resources, Inc.
6. + 7. Annual report for Lear Siegler, Inc. plus accompanying fact book and capabilities book.

SVE - CIA AN - TI - QUA

(Sve′ • sha Ann • tē′ • gwa)

4

5

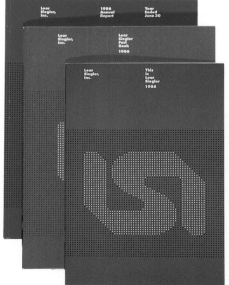

6

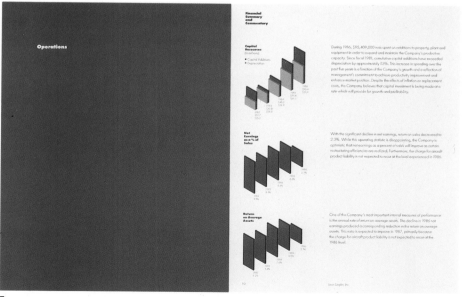

7

1

1. Coffee table book.
2. Point-of-purchase packaging for sun care products.
3. Annual report for Pacific Enterprises.
4.-6. Proposed graphics management program for U.C.L.A.
7. Symbol for Anderson Lithograph.
8. Symbol for Central Typesetting Company.
9. Symbol for Dacosystems.
10. Symbol for Don Quarrie and Associates.
11. Symbol for International Medical Exchange.

2

3

4

5

6

7

8

9

10

11

233

1. + 2. Annual report for
St. Francis Medical Center.
3. + 4. Annual report for Comprehensive Care Corporation.
5. + 6. Annual report for Eldon
Industries, Inc.
7. + 8. Annual report for Eldon
Industries, Inc.

1

2

3

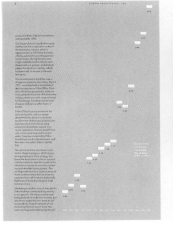

4

5

6

7

8

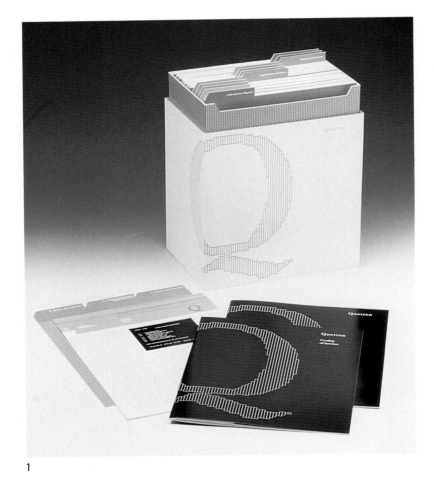

1

1. Packaging and informational brochures for Quotron.
2. Symbol and applications for Swett & Crawford, Inc.'s broker training program.

2

JAMES ROBIE DESIGN ASSOCIATES

Founded in 1978, this design firm is snugly placed between two fine art galleries. It's not wholly coincidental.

Designer James Robie is also a painter and sculptor who discovered he is just as comfortable in the boardroom as he is behind the easel. The result: corporate identity programs, logos, annual reports, posters, packaging and brochures are now his art.

He and his staff occupy the upper floor of a building Robie totally redesigned, reflecting his knowledge of environmental design and architecture.

Of his approach to business, Robie says, "We're service-oriented. I'm like a doctor —on call twenty-four hours a day."

1

2

5

3

6

4

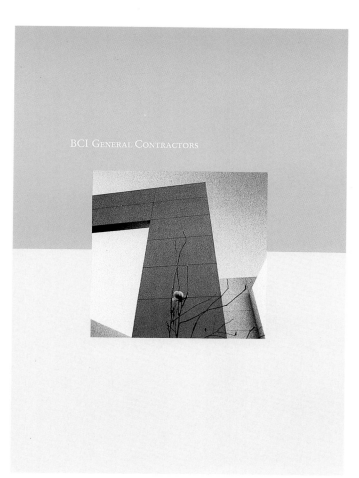

BCI GENERAL CONTRACTORS

7

1. James Robie.
2.-6. Materials created for the 1984 Olympics in Los Angeles including (2) "family" list, folder and identity cards, (3) one of twenty-three venue posters, (4) symbol for International Olympic Committee, (5) poster for sponsors, and (6) symbol for Patron ticket program.
7.+8. Capabilities brochure for Bedford Construction Company.

8

1

2

3

1.-6. "Wordmark" and applications for
TRW Credentials Service including
(2-5) brochures and (6) calendar.
7.+8. Capabilities brochure for a
developer.
9.+10. Brochure for Mitsubishi Motor
Sales of America.

4

5

6

7

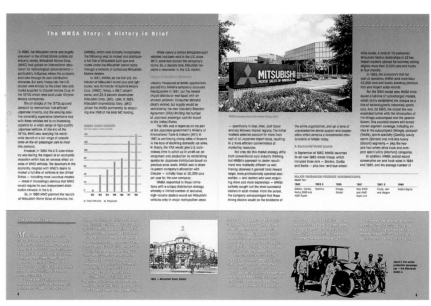

8

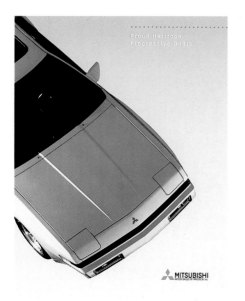

9

10

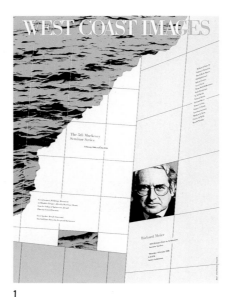

1

AN INTERNATIONAL SYMPOSIUM ON BLINDNESS AND VISUAL IMPAIRMENT IN LOS ANGELES, FEBRUARY 3-6, 1988

Everybody's Business

CO-SPONSORED BY THE AMERICAN FOUNDATION FOR THE BLIND AND THE FOUNDATION FOR THE JUNIOR BLIND

2

1. Poster for the Architecture Department at Cornell University.
2. Promotional poster for a symposium on blindness.
3. + 4. Invitation, folded and opened for the opening of a Japanese garden, entitled "Kimono on Over."
5. + 6. Annual report for the Foundation for the Junior Blind.
7. Symbol for Palm Desert Town Center.
8.-10. Gift certificate mailers for a supermarket.
11. + 12. Brochure for the U.C.L.A. Guest House.

3

4

FOUNDATION FOR THE JUNIOR BLIND ANNUAL REPORT

1 9 8 7

5

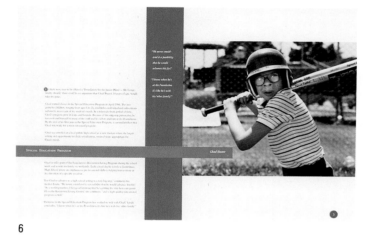

6

7

VONS PARTY PLATTERS

8

VONS GIFT BASKETS

9

11

12

VONS GIFT CERTIFICATES

10

1

2

3

4

1.+2. Capabilities brochure for Equidon.
3.+4. Capabilities brochure for Kaiser Aerospace and
Electronics Corporation.

ROBERT MILES RUNYAN & ASSOCIATES

Major corporate identity programs have long been a specialty of Robert Miles Runyan and Associates. From the 1984 Olympic Games to Vaurnet of France, the firm has created some of the most recognizable programs, here and internationally.

Situated in Playa del Rey, RMR&A is a full-service marketing and design company, providing research, strategic planning and creative development for a broad range of clients. Along with corporate identity, the firm also creates annual reports and environmental graphics.

Drawing on over thirty-five years' experience, Bob Runyan says, "The closer relationship you build with the chairman of the board, the better answers you're going to bring to their problems."

"The main thing," Runyan continues, "is to make the cash register jingle for the client."

1

1. Interior of studio.
2. Page from the graphic standards manual for the 1984 Olympic Games. The symbol for the games was designed by the studio.
3. + 4. Annual report for Compact Video.
5. + 6. Annual report for Transamerica Corporation.

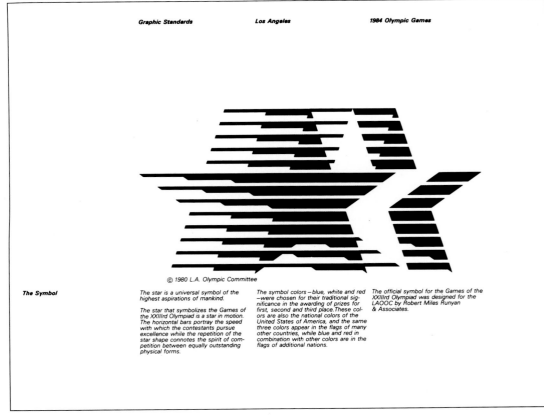

Graphic Standards   *Los Angeles*   *1984 Olympic Games*

© 1980 L.A. Olympic Committee

The Symbol

The star is a universal symbol of the highest aspirations of mankind.

The star that symbolizes the Games of the XXIIIrd Olympiad is a star in motion. The horizontal bars portray the speed with which the contestants pursue excellence while the repetition of the star shape connotes the spirit of competition between equally outstanding physical forms.

The symbol colors—blue, white and red —were chosen for their traditional significance in the awarding of prizes for first, second and third place. These colors are also the national colors of the United States of America, and the same three colors appear in the flags of many other countries, while blue and red in combination with other colors are in the flags of additional nations.

The official symbol for the Games of the XXIIIrd Olympiad was designed for the LAOOC by Robert Miles Runyan & Associates.

3

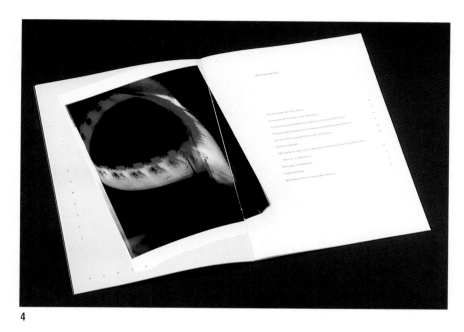

4

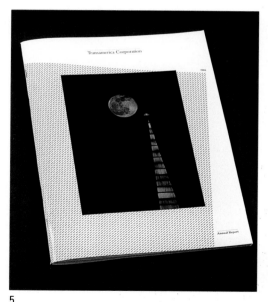

5

6

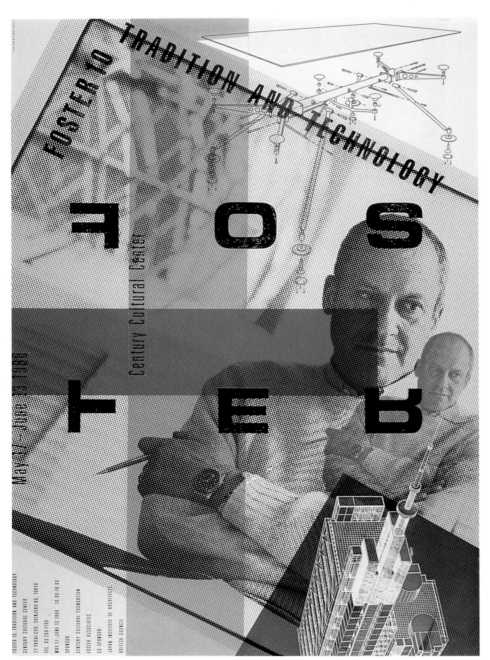

1. Poster for a lecture on architecture.
2. + 3. Annual report for Caremark, Inc.
4. Symbol for Caremark, a holding company comprised of three subsidiaries.
5. Symbol for Health Data Institute.
6. Symbol for America's Pharmacy.
7. Symbol for Home Health Care of America.

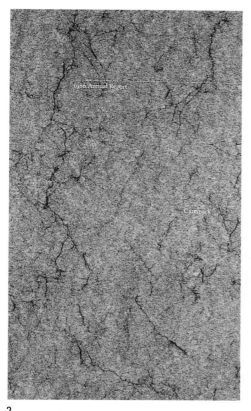

2

3

4

6

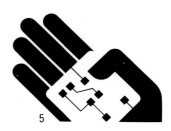

5

7

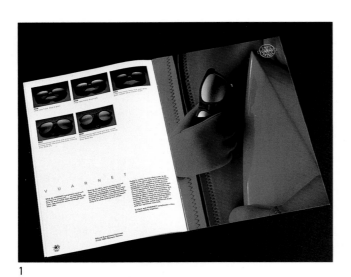

1

2

3

4

1. Catalog for an eyeglass manufacturer.
2. Stationery system for Sarsa.
3. Symbol and signage for Unibanco, a Mexican bank.
4. Signage and symbol for the city of Burbank, California.
5. Symbol for Obunsha, a Japanese publisher.
6. Logotype for Optima Retail Systems, Inc.
7. Symbol for Angeles.
8. Symbol for Unisource, Inc., a paper distribution company.
9. Symbol for Crown Zellerbach Paper Company.
10. Symbol for Los Angeles Rams 40th Anniversary.
11. Symbol for Vuarnet, France.
12. Symbol for Pharmavite, a pharmaceuticals manufacturer.

5

6

7

8

9

10

11

12

ROBERT MILES RUNYAN & ASSOCIATES
· ·

200 E. Culver Blvd.   Playa del Rey, CA 90293   213/823-0975 FAX: 213/823-0981

1

2

1. Packaging system for San'wiches.
2. Packaging system for Optima.

SHIFFMAN YOUNG DESIGN GROUP

1

Founded three years ago, this design firm prides itself on the fact that when you work with Shiffman/Young, you actually *work* with Tracey and Roland. They, along with a few hand-picked individuals, do all the work.

The work they do ranges from brochures to record covers to logo designs to educational materials. For clients representing disciplines from the arts to health sciences.

"We work with all kinds of people," says Shiffman. "We've even handled Invaders From the Beyond." Whatever the job is, the game plan remains the same. To solve the problem.

"Design firms are like football teams," explains Young. "They all go out with the same strategy. What separates them is that certain coaches win. Certain coaches lose."

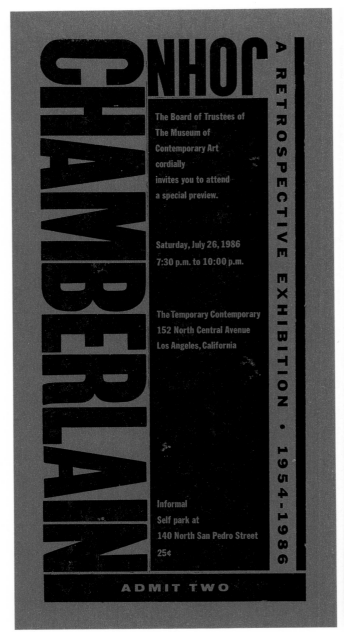

JOHN
CHAMBERLAIN

A RETROSPECTIVE EXHIBITION • 1954-1986

The Board of Trustees of
The Museum of
Contemporary Art
cordially
invites you to attend
a special preview.

Saturday, July 26, 1986
7:30 p.m. to 10:00 p.m.

The Temporary Contemporary
152 North Central Avenue
Los Angeles, California

Informal
Self park at
140 North San Pedro Street
25¢

ADMIT TWO

2

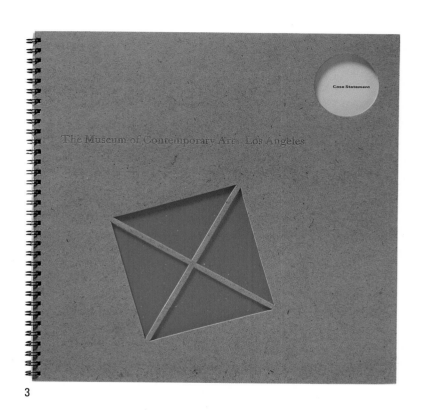

3

1. Tracey Shiffman, Roland Young.
2. Poster for The Museum of Contemporary Art, Los Angeles.
3.-5. Fundraising brochure for MOCA, Los Angeles. The brochure makes extensive use of irregular page sizes.

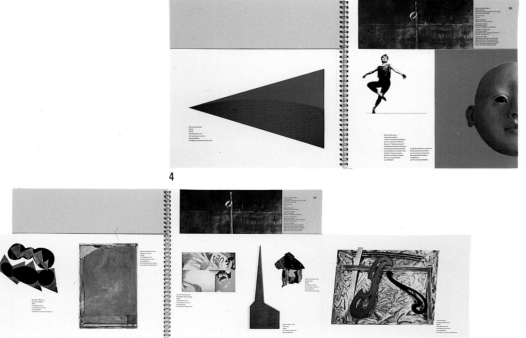

4

5

1

2

3

1.-3. Publications for Orthopedic Hospital Foundation.
4.-6. Annual report for Orthopedic Hospital Foundation.

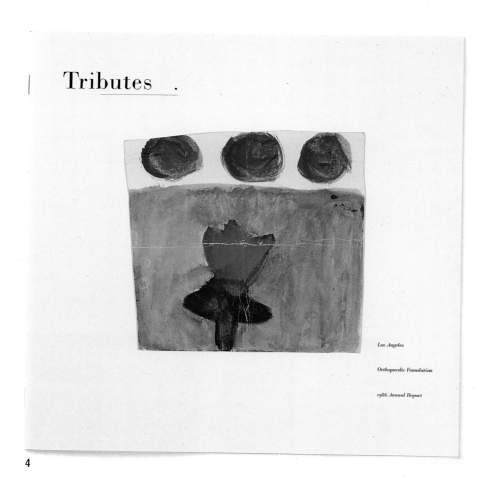

Tributes .

Los Angeles

Orthopaedic Foundation

1986 Annual Report

4

IS THE GLASS HALF EMPTY OR HALF FULL?

5

6

1

2

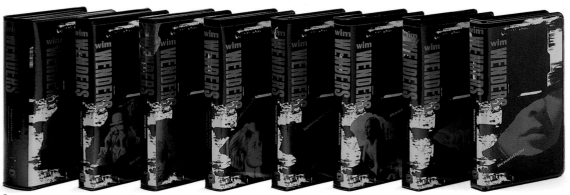

3

1. Poster and video package for Pacific Arts Video.
2. Packaging for The Complete Series of Beatles CD's for Capitol Records.
3. Packaging series for Pacific Arts Video.
4. Album design for Capitol Records. Sculpture by Michael C. McMillen.

SHIFFMAN YOUNG DESIGN GROUP

· ·

7421 Beverly Blvd., Suites 4 & 5   Los Angeles, CA 90036   213/930-1816, 213/930-1873

1

1. Identity system for The
Frederick R. Weisman Collection.
2. Catalog for Red Grooms/
Michael C. McMillen exhibit at
the Los Angeles Municipal Arts
Gallery.

260   2

PATRICK SOOHOO DESIGNERS

"We design solutions. Creative solutions that meet marketing and communication objectives. Simply. Effectively. Uniquely," says Patrick SooHoo.

To that end, the design firm becomes a partner with the client's marketing strategy. "Graphics is but one major element in an overall design program," comments Patrick.

Their work which ranges from package design to merchandising materials to identity programs, is formulated to fit into overall marketing programs, while still maintaining an exemplary creative spark.

"Design is more than making something look good," says Patrick, "It has to communicate, evoke a response or create an emotion."

2

1

3

4

5

7

1. (L-R) Stan Kassin, Jacqueline Moe and Patrick SooHoo.
2. Complete consumer check program for Bank of America.
3. + 4. 32-page newspaper insert created for California's Department of Tourism.
5. Logotype for a pizza chain.
6. + 8. Entire corporate communications program for Retirement Inns of America.
7. Symbol for Retirement Inns of America.

6

8

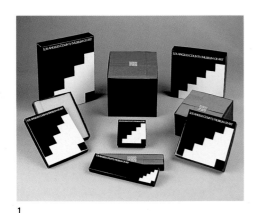

1

2

3

4

5

1.+**2.** Packaging for Los Angeles
County Museum of Art.
3. Packaging for single-serving
soft-boxed wine.
4. Symbol for Motherhood Maternity
stores.
5. Point-of-purchase display for
Wallace Berrie's toys.
6. Symbol for Mammoth Lakes Resort
Association.
7. Promotional "passport" for winter
visitors offering discounts and
premiums for summer.
8. Promotional materials promoting
year-round tourism for Mammoth
Lakes Resort Association.

6

7

8

1. Sales incentive materials for Executive Life Insurance.
2. Symbol for Larry's Deli.
3. + 4. Sales incentive materials for Executive Life Insurance.
5. + 8. Promotional poster for sales incentive travel promotion for LouverDrape.
6. Symbol for The California Egg Advisory Board.
7. Information System for Pioneer Electronics car division.
9. Student banking program kit for Bank of America.

1

2

3

4

6

5

7

8

9

1

1.-16. Pictograms for Pacific Bell White Pages Customer Guide.
1. Establishing Service
2. Emergency Crisis Hotlines
3. Community Services Hotline
4. How to Reach Us
5. Catalog of Services
6. Directory Services
7. Operator-Assisted Calls
8. Billing and Payment
9. Local and Nearby Calling
10. Service Areas
11. Long Distance Calling
12. International Calling
13. Your Rights and Responsibilities
14. Nuclear Guide
15. Paginas En Espanol
16. Our Liability, Your Responsibility

2

3

4

5

6

7

8

9

10

11

12

13

14

15

16

SUSSMAN/PREJZA & COMPANY, INC.

In 1984, Sussman/Prejza & Co. brought the world the Summer Olympic Games. It was an excellent example of what this firm refers to as "image design."

The Sussman/Prejza approach takes every element in an environment into consideration. In designing a retail project, for instance, the activities planned for the space are as important as the colors and materials used on the building facade or the project logo.

Deborah Sussman and her husband and partner, Paul Prejza, have traveled extensively and are drawn to festivals, local markets, indigenous graphics and architecture, and the integration of everyday life and design. It's this thoughtful and colorful view of the world that influences the firm's work.

1

2

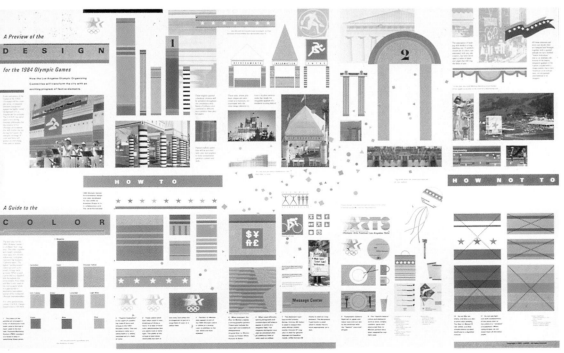

3

4

1. Deborah Sussman and Paul Prejza.
2. Logotype for 1984 Olympics.
3. Kit of Parts poster for the 1984 Olympics.
4.-7. Environmental graphics for 1984 Olympics.
8. + 9. Banners and program mailer for the Hollywood Bowl.

5

6

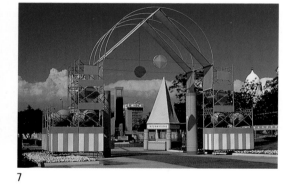

7

8

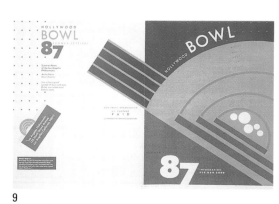

9

1. Neon symbol for Standard Shoes.
2. Interior environment for Standard Shoes.
3. Barricade for 6500 Wilshire.
4. Signing for 6500 Wilshire.
5. Symbol and logotype for Chicago Place.
6. Symbol for Canary Wharf, London.
7. Logotype for Howard Hughes Center.
8. Logotype for The Rand Corporation.
9. Logotype for Santa Monica Arts Partnership.
10.-13. Signing at Pacific Design Center, Los Angeles.
14.-18. Signing system, building color and banners for Crocker Center, Los Angeles.

1

2

3

4

CHICAGO
PLACE

5

6

HOWARD
HUGHES
CENTER

7

THE RAND CORPORATION

8

SMARTS
PARTNERSHIP

9

11

10

12

13

14

15

16

17

18

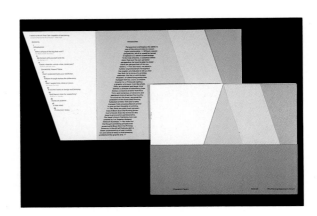

2

3

5

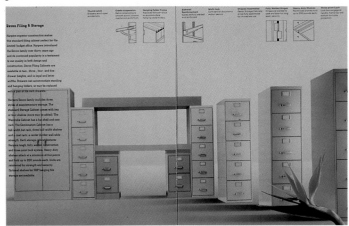

4

1. Promotional brochure for Champion
Paper Company.
2. Catalog for U.C.L.A. summer session.
3.+4. Proposed catalog and spread
for a furniture manufacturer.
5. Mailer for The Women's Building,
Los Angeles.
6.-10. Environmental design for
Hasbro, Inc.'s New York
Showroom.

7

6

8

9

10

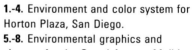

1

2

3

4

1.-4. Environment and color system for Horton Plaza, San Diego.
5.-8. Environmental graphics and signage for the Grand Avenue Mall in Milwaukee, Wisconsin.

5

6

7

8

Ken White, President and Creative Director of White + Associates, believes in becoming "personally involved right away to help a client assess needs and objectives and develop solutions that are both conceptually strong and highly creative."

Founded in 1968 and based in Los Angeles, White + Associates brings its marketing communications flair to clients throughout the U.S. and Europe. The firm responds to a wide range of client needs, from corporate identity programs and annual reports to packaging and environmental design.

The White vision increasingly reflects the personal statements which many companies are now making. "The personal, intensely human touch is a great counterpoint to the statistical marketing emphasis of recent years," White points out. "I anticipate becoming more absorbed in bringing those personal statements and styles to life."

1

white+Associates

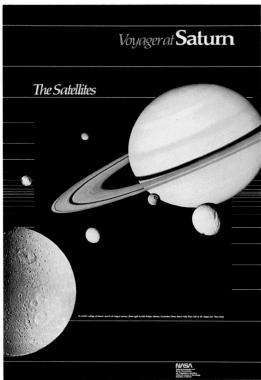

2

3

4

5

6

1. Ken White.
2. Catalog for Mead's Top Sixty
Competition.
3. Poster series for NASA.
4. Hangtag symbol for Hang Ten Kids
Swimwear.
5. Collateral sales material for
Hang Ten.
6. Promotional Poster for Hang Ten
Swimwear.

1

HETKERVEL

2

3

OROAMERICA

4

5

6

1. Symbol for the Los Angeles Graphic Arts Guild.
2. Symbol for a Dutch resort.
3. Symbol for Xidon, Inc., a data processing company.
4. Symbol for OroAmerica.
5. Symbol for Milk Maid, a personal care products line.
6. Hardcover book for NASA.
7. Corporate Identity program for Pacific Financial Companies.
8. Annual report for Pacific Financial Companies.
9. Poster for Lockheed.

7

8

9

281

1

2

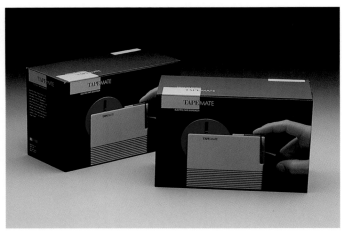

3

TAPE MATE

4

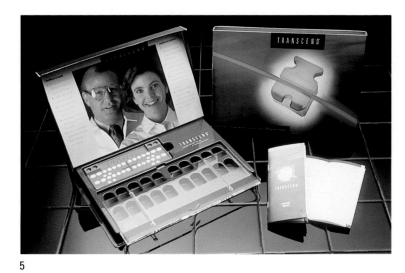

5

T R A N S C E N D

6

7

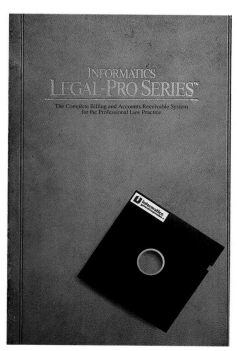

8

9

1. Promotional packaging for Club Dauphin.
2. Symbol for Club Dauphin, a beach club on the French Riviera.
3.+4. Packaging and logotype for Tapemate.
5.+6. Packaging and logotype for Transcend, translucent orthodontic braces.
7. Financial forecast for First Interstate Bank.
8.+9. Brochure for Informatics.

1

1. Corporate identity system for Hiebert Textiles and Hieberts Prism Furniture.
2. Signage and symbol for Country Life, a vegetarian buffet restaurant.

2

WILLIAMSON & ASSOCIATES

Dave Williamson and his designers create everything from collateral programs to packaging to environmental graphics to corporate identity to advertising.

They provide that work to a variety of industries—health care, foodservice, wine, electronics, furnishings and entertainment.

Founded twenty years ago, the company's expertise lies in direct-mail programs. ''Whether it's for one job or a long-term project, we're direct marketing specialists,'' explains Dave.

1

1. Dave Williamson, Christian Babcock and Vincent Pavelock.
2.-5. One of nine Olympic ticketing stores. Designed, fabricated and installed in shopping malls throughout Los Angeles in nine weeks.

2

3

4

5´

287

1

2

3

1. Catalog for gourmet foods.
2. + 3. Catalog for retailers for
Lorimar Home Video.
4. Corporate gift-buying system
for Blue Diamond Almonds.
5. + 6. Catalog for smoking and
gift accessories franchise.
7. Catalog for consumer
electronics.
8. Catalog for furniture
manufacturer.

4

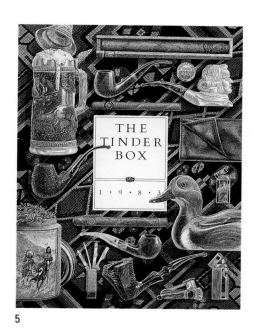

5

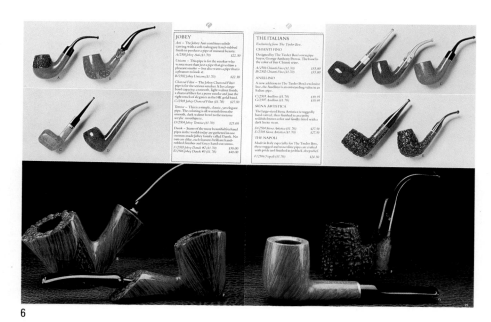

6

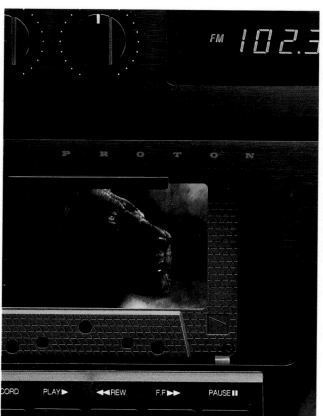

7

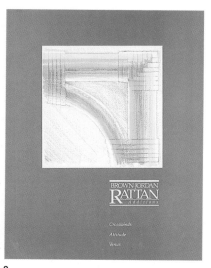

8

1. Packaging for Christmas self-promotion.
2. Packaging for a series which includes integral pop-ups. For Marvel Video Universe.
3. Packaging for "how-to" tapes for Kool-Aid/Lorimar.
4. Invitation to a charity event which includes a cassette with a personal invitation from Cary Grant and Barbara Walters.
5. + 6. Gift carton and individual packaging for Cartoon Classics from Disney.
7. Packaging and campaign system for Lorimar.

1

2

3

4

5

6

7

WILLIAMSON & ASSOCIATES

8800 Venice Blvd.   Los Angeles, CA 90034   213/836-0143 FAX: 213/836-0167

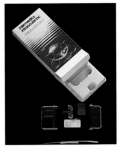

2

1

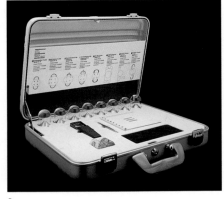

3

4

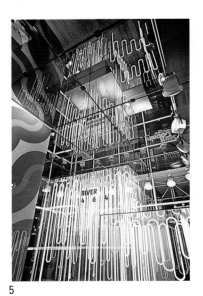

5

6

1. Traveling display for Intermedics.
2.-4. Components for an inter-ocular lens system including packaging and a portable presentation case.
5. Permanent industrial display for a French glass company, located in their Paris headquarters.
6. In-store point-of-purchase display for car racks which hold sporting equipment.

April Greiman, Inc.
April Greiman
620 Moulton Ave., #211
Los Angeles, CA 90031
213/227-1222 FAX: 213/227-8651

Hershey Associates
Christine Hershey, Jeffrey M. Natkin
3429 Glendale Blvd.
Los Angeles, CA 90039
213/669-1001 FAX: 213/669-0613

Huerta Design
Carlos Huerta, Hector Huerta, Octavio Huerta
3300 Temple St.
Los Angeles, CA 90026
213/381-6641 FAX: 213/738-8106

Wayne Hunt Design
Wayne Hunt
87 N. Raymond Ave., #215
Pasadena, CA 91103
213/257-2962, 818/793-7847 FAX: 818/793-2549

Intralink Film Graphic Design
Anthony Goldschmidt
155 No. Lapeer Dr.
Los Angeles, CA 90048
213/859-7001 FAX: 213/859-0738

The Jefferies Association
Ron Jefferies, Claudia Jefferies
430 S. Westmoreland Ave.
Los Angeles, CA 90020
213/388-4002 FAX: 213/388-4089

Rusty Kay & Associates, Inc.
Rusty Kay
209 Hill St.
Santa Monica, CA 90405
213/392-4569 FAX: 213/399-3906

Libera & Associates
Joan Libera
12020 W. Pico Blvd.
Los Angeles, CA 90064
213/477-2027 FAX: 213/477-9392

Scott Mednick & Associates
Scott Mednick
7412 Beverly Blvd.
Los Angeles, CA 90036
213/938-3839 FAX: 213/938-8950

Morava & Oliver Design Office
Emmett Morava, Douglas Oliver
204 Santa Monica Blvd.
Santa Monica, CA 90401
213/458-3588 FAX: 213/393-0987

James Robie Design Associates Inc.
James Robie
152½ N. La Brea Ave.
Los Angeles, CA 90036
213/939-7370 FAX: 213/937-9728

Robert Miles Runyan & Associates
Robert Miles Runyan
200 E. Culver Blvd.
Playa del Rey, CA 90293
213/823-0975 FAX: 213/823-0981

Shiffman Young Design Group
Tracey Shiffman, Roland Young
7421 Beverly Blvd., Suites 4 & 5
Los Angeles, CA 90036
213/930-1816

Patrick SooHoo Designers
Patrick SooHoo
8800 Venice Blvd.
Mezzanine, Suite A
Los Angeles, CA 90034
213/836-8800 FAX: 213/839-3039

Sussman/Prejza & Company, Inc.
Deborah Sussman, Paul Prejza
1651 18th St.
Santa Monica, CA 90404
213/870-4871 FAX: 213/829-7267

White + Associates
Ken White
137 N. Virgil Ave., #204
Los Angeles, CA 90004
213/380-6319 FAX: 213/380-3427

Williamson & Associates
Dave Williamson
8800 Venice Blvd.
Los Angeles, CA 90034
213/836-0143 FAX: 213/836-0167

GEM/F&C

mail list
call Tues

Vahé Fattal
Chairman of the Board

GEM/F&C
1119 Colorado Avenue
Suite 104
Santa Monica, CA 90401
658-9499

Stan Evenson Design Inc.

4445 Overland Avenue
Culver City, California 90230
213 204·1995

Stan Evenson

SM&A

Scott Mednick and Associates
Design and Advertising
7412 Beverly Boulevard
Los Angeles 90036-2796
213 .93

Sussman / Prejza & Company, Inc.

1651 18th Street

Santa Monica

California 90404

213 829 3337

FAX 213 829 7267

▲ Deborah Sussman
Principal

HUERTA DE

Carlos Huerta

3300 Temple Street
Los Angeles
California 90026

Telephone
Facsimile

8800
Venice
Boulevard
Mezzanine
Suite A
Los
Angeles
California
90034
213
836
8800

PATRICK SOOHOO
DESIGNERS
PREMIUM
DESIGN & MARKETING

L
and

**Design
Marketing
Communica**

Follis Design

Grant Follis

introduces the *foot long*

California **90004**

Los Angeles

April Greiman

301 **N** Gower

1   2   3   4   5

John Cleveland, Inc., 11611 San Vicente Boulevard

BOYD

Douglas Boyd

**Douglas Boyd
Design and Marketing**
A Division of
Primary Resources
Incorporated
8271 Melrose Avenue
Los Angeles, California
90046
Telephone
213 65

THE DE

351 EAST 6TH STREE

The Graphics Studio
North Highland
Angeles, California

ダイアー/カーン (株)

90036 カリフォルニア州
ロスアンゼルス
ウィルシャー ブルバード 5550
301号室

デザイン、広告

213 937-410

ロッドダイアー

社長

Josh Freeman
President

JOSH FREEMAN / ASSOCIATES

Marketing Design Group
8019½ Melrose Avenue, Suite 1
Los Angeles, California 90046
213 653 6466

HERSHE
3429 GLEN
LOS ANGE
13 669-1001

JEFFREY M. NATK
DESIGN DIRECTOR

ANTISTA DESIGN

1427 SANTA MONICA MALL
SUITE 206   SANTA MONICA,
CALIFORNIA 90401
-393-1352

...STA

K

RUSTY KAY

RUSTY KAY & ASSOCIATES, INC.,
209 HILL STREET
SANTA MONICA, CALIFORNIA 90405
(213) 392-4569

James Robie Design Associates

James Robie
President

152½ North La Brea Avenue
Los Ange...

41

213.
477-2027

...tes

Joan D. Libera

AD

Advertising Designers, Inc.   Thomas D. Ohmer
President

818 North La Brea A...
...ngeles
...rnia 90038-3...

Telephone
(213) 463-8143

213   462-1771   227-1222
10   11
9
8
7
...rd

Douglas Oliver

Morava & Oliver Design Office

204 Santa Monica Boulevard
Santa Monica, California 90401
Telephone: 213 458 3588

GNORY

ALMQUIST
...sident

GNORY INC.

BEACH, CA (213) 432-5707
90802

COY

...CIATES
...ULEVARD
...FORNIA 90039

CA 90232 213 837 0173

white + Associates

137 North Virgil Avenue
Suite 204
Los Angeles, California 90004

213 380-6319

Marketing Design
Communications

Ken white
President

Anthony Goldschmidt
President

INTRALINK
FILM
GRAPHIC DESIGN

155 North LaPeer Drive
Los Angeles, California 90048
Telephone 213 859-7001

Cover Photography:

Courtesy Art Directors
Club of Los Angeles.

RICK BRIAN SHOOTS 387-3017
555 SOUTH ALEXANDRIA AVENUE LOS ANGELES, CA 90020

HERSHEY ASSOCIATES
3429 GLENDALE BOULEVARD
LOS ANGELES, CALIFORNIA 90039
213 669-1001

R. CHRISTINE HERSHEY
PRESIDENT

Designer:

Business Card
Photography:

Los Angeles
Photography:

(213) 469 2992

LIVZEY

7611 Melrose Ave., Los Angeles, Calif. 90046
651-5630
BILL MILLER
PHOTOGRAPHY FOR ADVERTISING, ETC.

Typography:

SKIL-SET
t y p o g r a p h e r s
1320 Venice Boulevard
MANNY PAIVA   Los Angeles, CA 90006

213-749-8066

Photo Credits
Sussman/Prezja & Associates
Pages 270 & 271: 1, Victoria
Mihich; 2-9 A. del Zoppo.
Pages 272 & 273: 3, 4, 8, 9,
12-15 A. del Zoppo; 17,
Burton Pritzger.
Pages 274 & 275: 1, 3, 4
Steve Simpson; 2, Kyoko Tsuge.

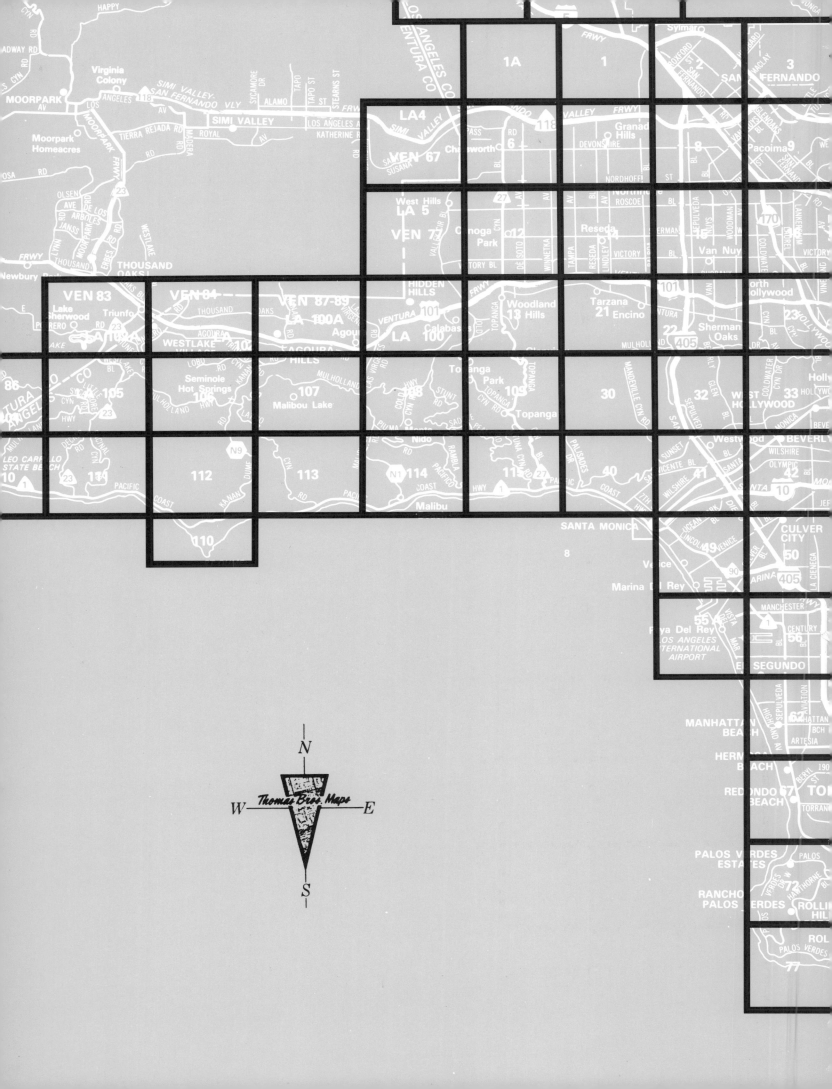